THE CONVICT SHIP,

A NARRATIVE OF THE RESULTS OF SCRIPTURAL INSTRUCTION AND MORAL DISCIPLINE ON BOARD THE "EARL GREY."

BY

COLIN ARROTT BROWNING, M. D.,

SURGEON, ROYAL NAVY.

From the Fourth English Edition.

WITH A PREFACE

BY THE REV. JAMES H. FOWLES,

RECTOR OF THE CHURCH OF THE EPIPHANY,
PHILADELPHIA.

"My people are destroyed for lack of knowledge."—HOSEA iv. 6.
"The gospel of Christ . . . is the power of God unto salvation to every one that believeth"—ROM. i. 16.
"It is the Spirit that quickeneth."—JOHN vi. 63.

PHILADELPHIA:
LINDSAY & BLAKISTON.
1850.

Entered, according to the act of Congress, in the year 1850, by LINDSAY & BLAKISTON, in the clerk's office of the District Court of the Eastern District of Pennsylvania.

W. S. YOUNG, PRINTER.

PREFACE TO THE AMERICAN EDITION.

This little volume will fill the heart of every benevolent reader with wonder and gratitude. Its author is an intelligent, pious and zealous Surgeon of the Royal Navy—who was placed in charge of some two or three hundred English convicts, during their transportation, on board the *Earl Grey*, to the penal colony of Van Diemen's Land. His work consists of a narrative, told in a perspicuous and interesting style, of a successful attempt to elevate these unpromising subjects out of that state of ignorance and sin in which they were found. The means employed were simple, yet enlightened, self-denying and kind; and their results are of a character so encouraging, that they will scarcely be anticipated by the believer, and cannot be understood by the infidel. At their debarkation, nearly all the prisoners could read the Word of God, and upwards of one hundred gave hopeful evidence of a change of heart. Nor were these hopes unfounded. In the Appendix, which consists of extracts from another production* of the same pen, in relation to this and similar voyages, will be found satisfactory proofs of the permanent and saving nature of that work of grace, which was begun on ship-board. The Comforter would indeed seem to have hovered over this vessel, as she pursued her long and trackless way upon the bosom of the deep, and to have imparted to a large portion of her refuse freight His richest blessings.

Dr. Browning's account of such unprecedented success among these outcasts has been very popular and effective in his own country; and it was thought that the republication of its Fourth English Edition here might serve many useful purposes.

Among other good ends, it may obviously contribute to such as these:—

The revival of a general confidence in the power of the simple Gospel, when accompanied by the Spirit of God, to renew and save the most abandoned and profane.

Is not our author's example, likewise, worthy of being held up for imitation before a Laodicean Church? His direct and zealous efforts for the glory of Christ, in the salvation of souls—his unmixed reliance upon the only appointed and effectual means,

* England's Exiles.

as they are recorded here with all singleness of mind, portray an instance of faith and love, which is but too rare in these days.

What valuable aid, also, may this volume afford to the pious visiters of our Penitentiaries, and Houses of Refuge! Such self-denying labourers will not only be encouraged by this narrative, but derive from it important suggestions in the prosecution of their work.

Place this book, moreover, in every convict's cell—and it will show that it is admirably fitted to inspire the wretched inmate with the best desires and hopes, and to point out to him a feasible, and tried, way of escape from the miseries in which he is involved.

On board of our immigrant ships, too, with such a modification as the circumstances would suggest to any pious officer, or influential Christian passenger, the system of doing good, which is here described, might in its main features be wisely introduced.

In short, there is scarcely any department of evangelical effort, that might not receive an impulse from what is recorded in these pages. There is no son or daughter of Adam, who may not be personally instructed, and profited by that work of God which is here disclosed. For the same change which these convicts experienced, must be wrought upon every fallen man, or he can never see the kingdom of heaven.* Except all repent, they shall likewise perish.† Unless all be washed in the blood of that Lamb, which was slain before the foundation of the world,‡ their sin cannot be taken away.§ It was in accordance with these Scriptural allusions, that a poet,|| whose character was as unexceptionable as that of any reader of these lines, sung—

> "The dying thief rejoiced to see
> That fountain in his day;
> And there may I, tho' vile as he,
> Wash all my guilt away."

And the London Christian Observer, in a favourable review of our work,¶ has well remarked: "Human nature, whether in towns or villages, in courts or cottages, in hospitals or prisons, in ships or camps, afloat or on shore, is essentially the same; corrupted by the same fall; needing the same remedy; and open by divine grace to the same blessed influences."

Philadelphia, February 1st., 1850.

* John iii. 3.   † Luke xiii. 1—5.   ‡ 1 Peter i. 18—20.
§ John i. 29. || Cowper.   ¶ April, 1847.

PREFACE.

When, in the year 1831, on being appointed to the *Surry,* the duties and responsibilities involved in the surgeon-superintendency of a convict ship, were, for the first time, imposed upon me, my inexperience of the nature of the service, and of the details of its duties, caused me no small degree of anxiety. I had, it is true, a copy of the printed official instructions; which gave a general view of my duties, but which supplied me with nothing like a scheme of education and discipline, and necessarily left the *minutiæ* of duty to my discretion.

Much of the time occupied by my first voyage, was expended in observation and experiment, and was therefore in some measure lost as to the moral improvement and instruction of the prisoners.

I entered on my second charge, in 1834, in the ship *Arab,* prepared with a system of instruction and government, the result of my experience, and to which some additions suggested themselves, during our progress to the Colonies. As my third voyage, in the *Elphinstone,* advanced, my plan received still farther improvements; and in this matured state it is now exhibited. Its fitness for the management of *female* convicts was ascertained in the year 1840; when (having in the mean time served in a ship-of-war) I accomplished, in the ship *Margaret,* my fourth voyage.

The narrative of the "*Convict Ship,*" depicts the happy results of this system in operation among 264 convicts, in my fifth voyage, on board the *Earl Grey;* and a still more abundant blessing attended my sixth and seventh voyages, in the *Theresa* and the *Pestonjee Bomonjee.*

My chief object in first publishing this volume, was the hope that it might supply some useful hints to officers engaging in the service to which it refers.

Several individuals, experienced in the Christian instruction of the neglected masses of our population, consider this system calculated to be useful, not only in convict ships, but, with suitable modifications, in emigrant ships, as well as in our country prisons and houses of correction: perhaps also in large manufactories.

We hear much in our days of the *separate, solitary,* and *silent* systems of prison discipline; but unless the CHRISTIAN system be brought to bear, with Divine power, on the understandings and consciences of criminals, every other system professedly contemplating their reformation, must, to the disappointment and confusion of its projectors, prove an utter failure. If we would see efficient moral discipline prevail in our prisons, penitentiaries, and convict hulks, we must provide for the effectual instruction of their inmates in the great facts and doctrines of Christianity; and must take care, that not only those intrusted with their religious instruction, but all who are connected with their management, from the governor down to the humblest warder, be spiritual and consistent Christians, fitted by their temper and general demeanour to commend the gospel of Christ to all around them.

We willingly concede to various systems of prison discipline their just measure of importance; but to expect that human machinery, however perfect, can take the place of God's own prescribed method of reformation, involves not only ignorant presumption, but practical infidelity.

To all who are intrusted with the education or government of human beings, in any rank or condition of life,—at sea or on shore; in the army, navy, or in civil life; in schools or private families,—the narrative contained in this volume may afford matter of interest, stirring them up to fervent prayer, and unwearied exertion in the work of scriptural instruction and Christian discipline, seeing that their labour shall not be in vain in the Lord; while the boundless riches of the grace of God in Christ Jesus, here displayed towards degraded criminals, may encourage sinners of every class to delay not, but hasten their flight to the one and only Refuge for the guilty, the defenceless and the lost.

It may be worthy of remark, that, on a review and comparison of my seven voyages, I find the amount of reformation amongst the convicts strikingly to correspond with the degree of diligence and zeal with which the gospel, in its *divine simplicity*, was brought to bear, from the hour of embarkation, upon their understandings, consciences, and hearts. During the first voyage, there was less of Christian instruction, and much less apparent improvement: on one occasion I was induced to yield to the judgment of the officer of the guard and master of the ship, and sanction the infliction of corporal punishment upon three convicts, which, how clearly soever *deserved*, I have ever regarded as unwise and impolitic, and as casting a stigma upon the management of my first charge. As experience grew, and practical Christianity was from the beginning relied upon, punishments of any kind became less and less called for; and during my last two voyages, not only were no lashes inflicted, but not an iron was used, nor a convict placed under a sentry.

To the honour of the blessed Saviour, who "hath done such great things for us," is this small and feeble work humbly and devoutly dedicated. May He forgive all that is *man's*, and abundantly bless all that is His own; and to the Father, the Son, and the Holy Ghost, the one only true God, be ascribed all glory, and honour, thanksgiving, dominion, and praise, now and evermore, world without end. *Amen.*

Bloomsbury-place, Brighton,
November 1*st*, 1848.

CONTENTS.

CHAPTER I.
                                                      Page.

Inspection and embarkation of the prisoners—Their moral position—Scriptural instruction the means of reformation 25

CHAPTER II.

State of the prisoners' education—Formation of schools—Subject-matter of instruction—The impressive position occupied both by the prisoners and the naval officer set over them 33

CHAPTER III.

Gratifying behaviour of the prisoners—Conversion to God the only foundation of true reformation—Some manifestations of spiritual change—A thunder-storm; its influence on the prisoners—Several profess faith in Christ—George Day—John Williams—A Socialist . 49

CHAPTER IV.

Account of W. B.—Special prayer—Converts increase—F. M.—J. S. 80

CHAPTER V.

More earnest prayer for the promised gift of the Holy Spirit—Hospital patients, J. H., W. C., T. G., and John Walker—Written statements from James B., Robert T., R. R——k 106

CHAPTER VI.

All Christians required to promote the knowledge of Christ—Reformed prisoners employed on this principle—Prayer and zealous labour to be conjoined—Death of Edward Marlow—Christmas Day—The Author receives a poisoned wound—Superior behaviour of the prisoners—Letters of J. W——n, T. C——y, and John M'D. . 131

CHAPTER VII.

Death of Abraham Button—Brief account of A. J., J. H., A. D., J. J., and others—Extracts from Journal continued—Resolution adopted by prisoners—Meetings for social prayer—Arrival at Hobart Town—Prisoners' address to the surgeon-superintendent—Number of apparent conversions—Farewell Address—Debarkation—A prisoner's letter 155

CHAPTER VIII.

Concluding statements—Summary of apparent good accomplished—Extract from a prisoner's letter, after he had been some time in the colony 181

APPENDIX 199

General outline of Scriptural instruction 227

Colonial Testimonies—concerning convicts by the "Earl Grey" and former ships 259

THE CONVICT SHIP.

CHAPTER I.

Inspection and Embarkation of the Prisoners—Their moral Position—Scriptural Instruction the Means of Reformation.

At Brighton, Sept. 3d, 1842, I had the honour to receive a letter, "on H. M. Service," from Sir John Barrow, Bart., Secretary to the Admiralty, acquainting me with my appointment as surgeon-superintendent on board the ship *Earl Grey*, destined to embark male convicts for the penal colony of Van Diemen's Land.

I instantly set about making the best possible provision for the education and instruction of the prisoners during the voyage, in addition to the religious books supplied by Government, by the aid of kind Christian friends and benevolent societies. On the 13th I received my instructions, joined my ship at Deptford, and directed the necessary preliminary arrangements for the approaching embarkation. On Saturday, the 17th, the ship dropped down to Woolwich; and on Monday, the 19th, ninety prisoners were inspected and embarked from the *Warrior* hulk, and ninety-four from the *Justitia*. The day following we sailed for Plymouth Sound, where we arrived on the 25th; and on the 26th, eighty prisoners were inspected and embarked from the hulk *Stirling Castle:* completing the number for whom accommodation had been prepared, namely, *two hundred and sixty-four* men.

The system of management which I had found, under the blessing of God, successful in five preceding voyages with convicts, I pursued from the first moment of entering upon my present charge.

Addresses were delivered to the prisoners after inspection, in the hulks,* which were listened to with breathless attention,—the men seemed to be brought at once under the moral influence of the system of management then referred to, and of the encouraging hope set before them: a hope calculated to generate moral life, to rescue from the chilling and destructive influence of despair, and to invigorate and prepare the mind for future usefulness and enjoyment.

The embarkation from the hulks took place exactly in the style I wished; with the solitary exception of one of the prisoners from the *Justitia* having been allowed by the petty officer in charge, to play his violin until the boat came within hail of my voice from the *Earl Grey*, when the ill-timed music was instantly stopped. Such a practice appeared to me to be highly indecorous, wholly at variance with the position of the prisoners, and of injurious influence, not only on *them*, but on all observers on shore,—espe-

* See Appendix.

cially that class of persons to which convicts belong. This incident became a subject of seasonable instruction, not only to the prisoners, but to the petty officer, who acknowledged on the quarter-deck that the fault was wholly chargeable on him, as he had *desired* the prisoner thus to act. Such embarkations as these, it is almost unnecessary to observe, ought ever to be conducted with the greatest possible solemnity.

The prisoners having been received on board, duly arranged, and disposed of in their respective berths, they were assembled on the quarter-deck and received their *first address* in the *Earl Grey*.*

But before we proceed farther with our narrative, it will be profitable to pause a little, and consider who they are that are thus assembled on the quarter-deck of a transport. Every one of these men is in possession of a spirit of immense value—a spirit on which He alone who called it into being can set the fair, the proper price: that price which He himself paid to redeem it from sin, pollution, and death, unto pardon, holiness, and life.

Let it also be remembered that these men, with very limited exceptions, are the victims of the darkest ignorance of Scripture truth; and although it would be unkind and destructive to the *prisoner himself* to palliate crime, and we are ever to regard all manner of sin, either in ourselves or others, with the most perfect abhorrence,—yet are we to look upon the transgressor with Christian pity and the tenderest

---

* See Appendix.

compassion, to recollect who it is that maketh us to differ, (wherein we do indeed differ!) and to bear in mind, that no man acquainted with the depths of deceitfulness in his own heart, as discovered in the light of God's word and Spirit, will take up the stone to throw at the convict. The man who, in the presence of the holy Lord God, can say to the prisoner, "Stand by thyself; I am holier than thou," gives but fearful demonstration of his own moral distance from God, and would probably be nearer the truth, were he to regard himself as more guilty and polluted in the sight of the Searcher of hearts, than the self-degraded and despised convict.

These prisoners assembled on the quarter-deck of the *Earl Grey*, have not only, however, in common with all men, violated the law of God, but they have despised and trampled upon the laws of their country, stained themselves with crimes committed against society and the state; rendered themselves a burden and a curse to those to whom they were bound to prove a help and a blessing,—and, notwithstanding all the untoward circumstances that may mark their lot in the world, some of them have heard the calls of the gospel and neglected the great salvation, while all have more or less resisted the light of reason and conscience. They are all, nevertheless, the "prisoners of hope." They form a portion of that family whom Christ came to *redeem* by his blood; for he came to seek and to save the lost; not to call the *righteous*, but *sinners* to repentance. The gospel of the grace of God reaches to them all, and is able to meet and to relieve the worst case which may be found amongst them.

It is only the spiritual knowledge of a crucified Redeemer that can inspire these men with hope, and make them worthy of our confidence, and safe and useful members of the community. "It is in vain," observes a distinguished servant of Christ, "to pluck the leaves off a tree; they will grow again: lay the axe to the root, and the leaves will all fall off, and will appear no more." Grappling with particular sins and vices merely, cannot warrantably be expected to produce any radical improvement of heart or reformation of life. To deal faithfully and effectually with men, we must begin where God in his word begins with them. We must clearly and impressively set before them their apostacy and depravity; their ignorance and utter helplessness; their need of a Divine and justifying righteousness, and the sprinkling of the blood of atonement. We must urge on their consideration the necessity of a change of heart, and the indwelling of the Holy Spirit, to produce in them, through the knowledge of Christ, that godly sorrow for sin which worketh repentance not to be repented of; to lead them into all Divine truth; to subdue their iniquities; and to cause them to love the Lord their God with all their heart, and soul, and strength, and mind, and their neighbour as themselves.

Accordingly, our first and grand object is to set before these men the inspired Scriptures. The voice which they require to hear is the voice of God the Spirit, speaking to their consciences and hearts from his word, convincing them of sin, of righteousness, and of judgment to come,—causing them to feel their guilt, to apprehend its deservings in the agonies of the worm that never dies; and giving them to perceive and feel the everlasting love of God manifested in the gift of his Son, that "*whosoever* believeth in him might not perish, but have eternal life." The outpouring upon them of that Spirit of promise is to be sought by believing, earnest, and persevering prayer. We must not be contented with moving on the surface. We must not be satisfied with attacking Satan's out-works. We must boldly, fearlessly, and in the spirit of the meek and lowly Jesus, assault the citadel. Thither must Divine truth be carried and immovably lodged by the Spirit of truth, the Lord of hosts; thence, by his almighty power, must the prince of darkness, with all that is unholy, be driven, and there must the Lord Jesus be enthroned.

Do these prisoners now, like the Jews of old, ask, "What shall we do that we might work the works of God?"* To that question the great Prophet of the church himself replies, "This is the work of God, that ye believe on Him whom he hath sent."† To believe on Christ is "the work of God;" not only because the faith that unites to Him, unto present and everlasting salvation, is the work of the Holy Spirit, but because *it is the beginning of all holy and acceptable obedience.* Until we receive Jesus, we are in a state of rebellion,—dead in trespasses and sins,—living not

---

* John vi. 28, 29.   † Ibid.

only in habitual violation of the Divine law, but in the act of rejecting the Son of God, the only Saviour from sin and wrath, resisting the Holy Spirit, and putting away from us that perfect salvation which Jesus accomplished, and is ever, in His Word, urging upon our *immediate, thankful* and *cheerful* reception. Without faith in Christ it is impossible to please God; and it is by faith in Christ Jesus that we become His children,* and are enabled to render Him acceptable service. Coercion, and even punishment, may, through the sinful neglect and rejection of the gospel, *become necessary* to restrain the evil passions and arrest the lawless and destructive career of man; but it is not by such means, or by any apparatus of man's construction, physical or moral, that the heart can be brought back to God, or men be qualified for fulfilling the offices of social life. God has shown us in His written word what is necessary to accomplish these great and paramount objects: and let us beware of presumptuously attempting to accomplish any one of them by other means than those of Divine appointment.

The period allotted to the voyage to the penal colonies, when rightly improved, is most favourable, under the Divine blessing, to the reformation of the guilty, and their recovery to God and to happiness; therefore the instruction and discipline of the people, according to the Scriptures, in the exercise of fervent and believing prayer, is to begin with their embarkation, and to be continued during the whole of the passage. Should

* Heb. xi. 6; Gal. iii. 26.

I, as the officer intrusted by Government with the "*entire management*" of these men—in opposition to my instructions from the admiralty, neglect thus to improve this opportunity, with a view to their reformation and happiness, I should prove myself unworthy of the confidence reposed in me, and inflict a great injury on souls, and therefore upon my country.

CHAPTER II.

State of prisoners' education—Formation of schools—Subject-matter of instruction—The impressive position occupied both by the prisoners and the naval officer set over them.

On the day immediately following that of their embarkation, the prisoners were assembled again on the quarter-deck to receive their *second* Address;* and various preliminary and necessary arrangements having been made, we forthwith proceeded with our system of organization.

The earliest opportunity was embraced to ascertain, by a close and personal examination, how the people stood as to their ability to read and write; and the following is the result:

Read and write, 53; read only, 23; read a little, 65; know their letters, 45; ignorant even of the alphabet, 77.

Therefore, in a very limited sense of the expression, there were found—educated, 76; uneducated, 187.

The prisoners were now formed into *twenty-four schools;* the *two* highest of which consisted of those who could read and write; the *third*, of those who could read only; *six*, of such as could read a little; *five*, of those who knew their alphabet; and *ten*, of such as did not know their letters.

* Appendix.

The schools having been fully organized, and teachers and inspector appointed, the whole of the prisoners were assembled on the quarter-deck; the inspector and schoolmasters were drawn up in lines, and placed before their pupils, when they were all addressed with reference to the new and interesting relations in which they now stood to each other as teachers and pupils.

Nothing could be more deeply interesting than the appearance which our decks now presented, above and below,— all was order, life, and activity. The hum of twenty-four schools, containing 263 pupils, from seventeen to fifty-eight years of age, had an effect upon my ear far surpassing that of the finest music. Wherever a school could be conveniently assembled, there the busy group were to be seen surrounding their teacher, eagerly vying which each other in application and zeal. There was of course great diversity of *aptitude,* both in communicating and receiving instruction; but almost every countenance betrayed thoughtfulness and attention, and was soon lighted up with more or less of hopeful animation. The diligence and zeal with which the prisoners in the *Earl Grey* set about the acquisition of useful knowledge, as well as the ability to read, exceeded any thing of the kind I have ever witnessed.

While learning to read, they were at the same time, acquiring useful knowledge also; for all our schoolbooks were instructive, and the sacred Scriptures were used from the beginning by several of the schools, and by all of them as the voyage advanced. An abundant variety of religious tracts, and of valuable little works published by the Tract Society, were in constant circulation, and diligently perused; by the great body of the people who could read when they embarked, and by others as they acquired the ability, were the Scriptures studied in private: morning and evening they were read publicly to the whole of the people assembled, and they were made the subject of catechetical examination, and of solemn and faithful exhortation, every evening, and as often in the morning as other duties admitted.

On the Lord's day, the prisoners were always assembled for "church" at 10 o'clock, A. M.; and as on former occasions, the first and second lessons were selected with reference to their present circumstances. Our sermons were selected from four volumes by the Rev. Charles Davy, which uniformly secured the most listening attention. At 2 o'clock, P. M., we met again, as during preceding voyages, for the recital of portions of Scripture, catechetical instruction, and exhortation. The number of men who gave in their names for public recitation, and repeated weekly their chapters to their respective schoolmasters, was considerable. Of course, our time did not permit *me* to hear the whole of these volunteers; I was compelled to rely on the testimony of the teachers and inspector,—who, I believe, never attempted to deceive me,—and to call upon as many to stand up and recite the passage assigned them, as our time would permit. The Old Testament types were often explained at the afternoon service, and they furnished the most clear and impressive illustration of the great doctrines of Christ and of His cross. The "singing of psalms and hymns, and spiritual songs," had its proper place in our public worship on the Lord's day, as well as in our daily social and devotional exercises.

It is difficult to imagine any spectacle more impressive than that of 263 outcasts, consigned by the violated laws of their country to all the horrors of transportation, closely seated on the quarter-deck of a transport, under sail to a remote quarter of the earth, with scarcely a hope ever again to tread their native shores, or to behold, in the flesh, those who are the dearest to their hearts,—and the ship's company, the soldiers, their wives and children, all in their sabbath day's costumes, arranged in their proper places on deck, all seriously engaged in the solemn worship of the Most High. There is something in the appearance of such a congregation which I am not able to describe, and the recollection of which is, at this moment, most touching to my feelings. The diversity of countenance, age and apparent character, among the prisoners; the soldiers under arms; the ship's crew, with their officers; the women and their children; all contributed to increase the interest, and add to the solemnity of our engagements. No congregation could exhibit more decided marks of extreme attention. Almost every countenance bespoke a mind engaged, and more or less impressed, especially those of the prisoners; and if at any time the attention of a prisoner seemed doubtful, an observant look, accompanied sometimes with a short pause, was sufficient to recall it.

SUBJECT MATTER OF INSTRUCTION. 37

Our prisoners were now in daily and constant contact with Divine truth; they were the subjects of earnest prayer—secret, and in their presence: the Holy Spirit* was, by means divinely appointed, graciously striving with their understandings, their consciences, and their hearts, and bearing witness to Christ, the Almighty Saviour of sinners, who waits to be gracious, and rejoices to pardon and to save. The whole counsel of God was, in the Scriptures, declared to them.

To the prisoners in the *Earl Grey*, though guilty rebels against God, he had commanded his overtures of forgiveness, reconciliation, and life, to be proclaimed as freely as to the rest of mankind. In the first epistle of John, it is written, "And this is His commandment, that we should believe on the name of His Son, Jesus Christ, and love one another, as he gave us commandment."† Oh, how merciful, how unutterably gracious is this *command of God* laid on *all* sinners before whose eyes Christ Jesus is set forth according to the Scriptures, *that they look unto him and be saved!* ‡—saved from sin and from death, unto holiness and life. How completely does such a Divine command strip all sinners of every plea they can possibly urge in defence or in palliation of their unbelief,—of their refusal to put on Christ as all their salvation and all their desire. However desperate their case may be, they are commanded

---

* Throughout this chapter, and elsewhere, our excellent author inseparably connects the Holy Spirit and the written or preached word, in a way, which has no authority from Scripture, or experience, and is, moreover, liable to some grave objections. J. H. F.

† 1 John iii. 23. ‡ Isa. xlv. 22.

of God to receive his beloved Son for pardon and peace, purification and life. How desperate soever their case may be, their refusal to believe on Jesus renders it still more desperate; their final rejection of Christ is their ultimate and unalterable resolve to perish for ever!'

At *what time* is God's command, that we receive Christ, to be obeyed? Does the Divine authority allow any delay? Do our desperate circumstances as sinners sentenced to death—to eternal death, and every moment liable to suffer the full execution of that awful and just sentence, in any degree favour delay? Does not every moment's delay aggravate our guilt and our danger? It was with these men as it is with any other body of people assembled in any place, whether at sea or on shore, where Christ, the unspeakable gift of God, is scripturally set before them; not an individual amongst them can quit the place which he occupies but in one of two characters; either that of a man who has been induced to throw down the weapons of his rebellion, to comply with the overtures of his rightful and benignant Sovereign, accept the Son as his divine surety and his peace, and so enter upon an interminable course of holy and cheerful obedience: or he retires, still clad in the armour of his apostacy, a rejecter of mercy, because a rejecter of Christ; more opposed to God than before; more hardened, more guilty, more dead; more unlikely ever to return to God by the reception of his Son.

The command of God to every sinner to whom His

gospel is published is, that he do *immediately* believe it. His inspired words are, "Behold *now* is the accepted time; behold *now* is the day of salvation."* The proclamation of the gospel of the grace of God knows nothing of to-morrow,—nothing of the next hour, in respect of the sinner's duty to believe it. To-morrow may come—the next hour may come, and to me there may be no gospel. This night my soul may be required of me! The next hour may leave me in that place where there is nothing but the fiery blackness, and darkness, and tempest; the ceaseless consciousness of *that guilt which I refused to wash away in the precious and atoning blood of Christ*, —the intolerable, but never-failing remembrance of a despised, rejected, and benignant Saviour!

Only mark our blessed Lord's lamentation over Jerusalem: " O Jerusalem, Jerusalem, thou that killest the prophets, and stonest them which are sent unto thee; how often would I have gathered thy children together, even as a hen gathereth her chickens under her wings, and ye would not."† Why perished these "murderers of the prophets?" Because they refused to receive the Messiah; and in rejecting Him they rejected pardon, peace, and life. And why do sinners *now* perish under the sound of the gospel? Because they choose to imitate them in rejecting Christ. They refuse to be gathered by the good Shepherd into his fold, to enjoy the security and bliss of his protection and smile for ever. Still it is true that the " *would I* " of Christ invites the sinner to come to him; and

* 2 Cor. vi. 2. † Matt. xxiii. 7.

makes it binding on his conscience to look to him and be saved. And the most desperate ingredient in the sinner's rebellion,—the most appalling feature in his character, is the wayward and criminal "*would not*," which he continues to oppose to the most merciful and gracious "WOULD I" of the Son of God? While the unbelieving sinner passes along to the gates of death, the compassionate "*would I*" of the Lord Jesus Christ ceases not to follow him to the very verge of time; and he enters into eternity to take his place among the unbelieving and undone associates of his choice, still opposing his desperate and ruinous "*would not*," to the long-suffering and gracious "*would I*" of our Divine Emanuel!*

The people gathered together in the *Earl Grey*, from all parts of the kingdom, are not only, in common with all men, urged to flee at once to the Lord Jesus Christ as the only refuge for the guilty and the lost, but, being now placed in circumstances peculiarly favourable to their instruction and reformation, they are the more emphatically called upon to avail themselves, without delay, of their inestimable privileges, at once to yield a believing obedience to the gracious calls of Divine mercy, and turn their feet into the path of holiness and life. In placing themselves in the position of convicts, they have voluntarily degraded themselves to an extent which defies all language to express, and the moral influence of their degradation, and of the circumstances by which they will be encompassed in

---

* See the effect of this text on the mind of a Socialist, chap. 3.

the colony, if not overruled by scriptural instruction and prayer, and the gracious operation of the Holy Spirit, will tempt them to give themselves up to the power of sin and of Satan, and willingly to seal their eternal destruction. There is, therefore, no time to be lost. They are hastening to a colony where the elements of spiritual and eternal death abound, and where there are but few of the elements of spiritual and everlasting life. But more than this: these men are on their way to death—to judgment—to eternity; they must sustain for ever the character in which they die, and experience all the misery or the bliss involved in that character, whether it shall be that of the unrenewed rejecter of Christ, or the regenerated and sanctified believer in His name; according as it is written, "He that is unjust, shall be unjust still; and he who is filthy, shall be filthy still; and he that is righteous, shall be righteous still; and he that is holy, shall be holy still."*
Impurity and guilt must be ever linked with wretchedness, and pardon and holiness with peace. Not only are these men on their way to death, judgment, and eternity, but *I*, too, hasten on with them—thither do I accompany them. With them, I must appear before the judgment-seat of Christ, to answer for the fidelity with which I watch for their souls, as well as for my own, and improve the opportunity afforded me of winning these my fellow-sinners to Jesus, and to a participation in the blessings of His great redemption.

* Rev. xxii. 11.

The eyes of men are upon them—the eyes of angels are upon them—the all-seeing eye of God is upon them! They are the subjects of a mighty contest. Satan desires and labours to retain and hold them fast in his bondage, that they may share with him in the pains of eternal fire. The Lord Jesus, who created and redeemed them, and whose property they are, seeks their confidence and their hearts; desires to rejoice over them as his ransomed, liberated, and sanctified children, the trophies of his victory over sin and Satan, and to present them to the Father with exceeding joy. And the contest of which these men are the subjects cannot terminate without the exercise of the *will* of each one of them. If they continue the slaves of Satan, they *choose* so to continue; they *prefer* his slavery before the Redeemer's liberty. If they renounce Satan, and become the faithful followers of Christ, they give themselves to Him willing with a *willing mind*. His love constrains them; they see the glory of Jesus, and believe on Him; they willingly and gladly choose him for their Lord and Saviour, and rejoice as giving themselves to him to be "formed for himself, for showing forth his praise." Their salvation, from first to last, they attribute to his rich and free grace; and to the Father, the Son, and the Holy Spirit, they, with devout and grateful ardour, for ever ascribe all the glory and all the praise.

From the commencement of the voyage to its termination, the prisoners breathe a moral and a spiritual atmosphere. They are in constant contact with Divine truth; God, as revealed in the gospel of His Son, is continually set before them, together with the great realities of time and eternity. Christianity—*Bible* Christianity, is kept perpetually in their view. Every hour carries its report to heaven! every hour records there the decision of every mind! The people are taught that God sends to each one of them a message —a message to which they cannot possibly fail every moment to reply, and the reply of each is either in accordance with, or in opposition to, the Divine will! From the question they cannot escape for a day or an hour, "*What answer do you purpose to give to the message of God?*" "What answer are you giving, and giving every instant?" The Holy Ghost is striving with each of them,—convincing them of truth, testifying to them of Christ and his great and finished salvation, and persuading them to choose, and to choose *now*,—the things which belong to their peace, lest they should be for ever hidden from their eyes; and to his gracious influences they willingly yield, or they wickedly resist them—and, persevering in their wilful resistance, they must ultimately quench the Spirit, and so destroy themselves under an accumulated load of aggravated guilt.

With the true nature of the salvation of Christ they become more and more familiarized; they are taught that it is a salvation not merely from hell— from wrath—from the remote consequences of sin; but a *present* salvation from guilt and impurity—from the love, power and practice of all manner of sin: a salvation to holiness of heart and life,—a salvation unto God! They are taught to maintain a watchful and spiritual discipline over their feelings and affections, their tempers and dispositions, their looks and manners, their words and conduct. All unholy selfishness and contention, all unjustifiable noisiness and unhallowed strife, are to be for ever banished from amongst them. They are now to become meek and lowly followers of the Lamb: the time past of their life is to suffice to have wrought the will of the flesh.

In seeking to win souls to Christ, it is absolutely necessary that our minds be deeply impressed with the scriptural truth of man's spiritual deadness and dislike to God and his truth, as well as of our own utter inability to convey to the mind of a fellow sinner a single spiritual thought.

The grand instrument which God hath been pleased to ordain for effecting man's conversion to himself, is the truth concerning Jesus, as set forth in the holy Scriptures.* The Lord hath, both by precept and approved example, required† all his believing people to make known the gospel of his grace to perishing sinners, as opportunity is afforded; and has graciously promised concerning His word, "It shall not return unto me void; but it shall accomplish that which I please, and it shall prosper in the thing whereto I send

* 1 Pet. i. 23; James i. 18; Eph. i. 13; 1 Thess. ii. 13, 14; John vi. 63; Jer. xxiii. 29; Acts viii. 1—4; Rom. x. 17; 1 Cor. i. 24.

† Prov. xi. 30; Isa. lii. 7; Dan. xii. 3; 2 Tim. ii. 24—26; James v. 19, 20; Rev. xxii. 17; Psalm xcvi. 2, 3; cv. 1; cxlv.; Numb. x. 29; 2 Kings v. 3, &c.; John i. 35—51; iv. 4—42: Acts viii. 4; Matt. xiii. 31—33; Mark v. 1—20; James v. 19, 20; Matt. vii. 12; v. 16.

it."* But even the inspired word of God concerning Jesus Christ and him crucified, derives its saving efficacy from the accompanying influences of the Holy Spirit. The gift of the Holy Spirit is the great promise of God to His Church;† spiritual illumination, conversion of heart unto God, vital union by faith to Christ Jesus, is His sole and peculiar work.

How impressive is this view of the state and condition of the prisoners in the *Earl Grey!* How impressive and humbling this view of our own agency! How necessary to wrestle without ceasing, in earnest and believing prayer, for the outpouring of the Holy Spirit upon ourselves, and upon all the people whom we seek to instruct and to win to Christ! How much is involved in this work of proclaiming Christ! how much that relates to the glory of God and the eternal welfare of souls! Oh! it is sacred, impressive, self-instructing, and most responsible work, to be moving, as it were, between time and eternity, between heaven and hell, between God the Saviour and Satan the destroyer, with reference to the salvation of our fellow-men! With a heart oppressed with a sense of its own unworthiness, and utter inability to afford saving aid to men, who are themselves not only helpless, but appallingly indifferent to spiritual deliverance; to visit

---

* Isa. lv. 10, 11.

† Isa. liv. 13; Jer. xxxi.; Joel ii. 28—32; Ezek. xxxvi. 27; xxxvii. 13, 14; Luke xxiv. 49; John vi. 63; iii. 3—8; xiv.; xvi.; Acts x. 44; ii.; Zech. iv. 6; 1 Cor. iii. 1—17; ii. 4, 5; 2 Cor. iv. 3—7; John iv. 23, 24; Gal. v. 16—25; Rom. viii. 9—16; Phil. i. 19; 1 Thess. i. 5, 6.

often the throne of Divine mercy and implore the outpouring of the Spirit upon these men; devoutly to look up for an answer of peace, and earnestly to watch for indications in their temper and conduct, of their reception or rejection of the gospel; to go again and again to the throne of grace, to pour out the heart to God, and in the dust to indulge either in humiliation and bitter lamentation, or devout praise, according as the Holy Spirit shall appear to be yielded unto or resisted! Oh, it is solemn work to be thus continually approaching God with reference to guilty men, under a deep impression of the nature of sin—the sufferings and death of Christ—the agonies inseparable from the eternal consciousness of guilt, that especially of rejecting God's "unspeakable gift," together with the joy, peace, and everlasting bliss which the believing reception of Christ secures! Oh, it is holy and peculiar work, to be continually coming to Jesus for a word of instruction—a message of mercy from His inspired Scriptures to the souls whom He hath made and redeemed; to be as often returning to the footstool of His throne, in bended lowliness of heart to tell Jesus, like the disciples of old, what we have done; and to leave the people and His truth in His own hands, imploring Him to glorify His name, and magnify the riches of His grace, in their present and everlasting salvation!

Many and fervent, without doubt, were the prayers offered up unto God in behalf of these men in the *Earl Grey,* by his believing people in many parts of England, Scotland, and Ireland, especially by those who so liberally supplied them with books, and by pious persons accquainted with individual cases among them. We are assured that the Lord Jesus hath entered into the holiest of all, in heaven, with His own blood, having obtained eternal redemption for us, and that He shall see of t hefruit of the travail of His soul, and be satisfied. We know that His grace is omnipotent—that His blood hath power to cleanse from all sin: it is manifest that the redemption which is sufficient to meet the case of *any* sinner, is fully adequate to meet the condition of the sinners embarked in the *Earl Grey;* and therefore we look and wait for Divine results amongst our isolated and now instructed exiles. Will Jesus illustrate the efficacy of His atonement, and the power of His word and Spirit, in the conversion and salvation of some, or many, or all of these men? For what great purpose, having been brought together in the *Earl Grey*, are they instructed in the way of pardon, holiness, and life? Will not the Lord, in His wisdom and mercy, overrule all their wickedness for good? Would not such a result be in harmony with the history of the Divine dispensations, and the immutable principles of the Divine government? May not God magnify the riches and the freeness of His grace, by plucking these men as brands from the fire; and so remind us, that no flesh shall glory in His presence, but that whosoever glorieth shall glory only in the Lord? Shall there be joy in heaven over some of these prodigals *brought to themselves*, and returned to their heavenly Father? Jesus is willing to save them; will they be made willing under the Divine influence of His manifested willingness, and of His everlasting and unchanging love? Oh the intensity of the interest that is felt by the faithful in these men! How vast their influence on the souls of other immortals! How inconceivable the influence of their decisions on the moral universe!

CHAPTER III.

Gratifying behaviour of the prisoners—Conversion to God the only foundation of true reformation—Some manifestations of spiritual change—A thunder-storm—Its influence on the Prisoners—Several profess faith in Christ—George Day—John Williams—A Socialist.

We now proceed to record the effects produced, under the Divine blessing, by our system, in the character, the tempers, and the general conduct of the prisoners during the voyage. In the *Earl Grey*, not only did the number of instances of individual reformation and apparent conversion to God exceed those which occurred in any of my former ships, but the behaviour of the people, *as a body*, surpassed any thing I had ever witnessed in any class of men at sea. From the day of their embarkation—indeed, from the hour of our first interview in the hulks, these men were manifestly under the influence of an intellectual and moral, if not of a *spiritual* power.

One man who had been, contrary to my regulations, put in circumstances of temptation, had his irons replaced for a given period, for theft and drunkenness; three youngsters, who, impelled, as they alleged, by an unwarrantable curiosity, were found to have quitted their proper place on the decks, were also for several days subjected to the degradation of having their irons replaced; one man, for incorrigible and most pernicious *levity*, was dismissed from his office of schoolmaster, and was repeatedly separated from the rest of the people; another man, who had been detected in using improper language, was once or twice placed in a state of separation ; and there were two or three of peculiar and excitable temper, with whom it was found necessary to deal oftener than once, on account of a tendency to indulge, during the first part of the voyage, in noisy disputation, which, though of momentary duration, can never be permitted to pass without an adequate expression of disapprobation and wholesome rebuke. But with the exception of *seven*, who might, perhaps, be justly pronounced indifferent characters, and from 13 to 19 more, with whom I was in some respects dissatisfied, no impropriety of conduct appeared amongst the whole 264 prisoners worthy of notice. On two or three occasions a few of them manifested a disposition to *slackness*, or other irregularity in the performance of duty, which gave rise to practical addresses, and impressive appeals to the understanding and conscience, with a view not only to the benefit of the individuals in fault, but that of all the people : and perhaps some of our most useful lectures were founded upon similar incidents manifesting some want of principle, or imperfection of character; but the general conduct of the prisoners was uniformly so superior, that the mere allusion to these very few exceptions tends to throw too dark a shade over the picture, and prevents the reader from distinctly perceiving the delightful order and harmony, the animating diligence and industry which every where pervaded our prison, both above and below; the studious attention of the people to our established regulations; and their courteous consideration and brotherly kindness, in all the relations in which they stood to one another, whether as petty officers and men, schoolmasters and pupils, or fellow-prisoners and fellow-sufferers.

Not only was the general behaviour of the prisoners from the beginning remarkably pleasing, but a thoughtful seriousness obviously pervaded them, which intimated that more was going on in their minds and hearts than was yet fully manifest, and which encouraged the most hopeful expectation. It was not mere outward decorum and correctness of moral deportment that could satisfy our mind, not a mere superficial reformation of speech and manners; we desired to see *that change* effected which would ensure future good conduct upon right and divinely-approved principles—that change which involves the safety and happiness of the soul in a future world, as well as consistent behaviour and usefulness in the present; our hearts' desire and prayer was, that the whole of our prisoners might be, by the power of the Holy Ghost, converted unto God, through the knowledge and faith of His beloved Son. While, therefore, our daily observation was watchfully and anxiously directed to the whole of the people, it took especial cognizance of those individuals whose temper and conduct gave any indications of spiritual life; and such observation gave an interesting, arousing, and useful turn to our occasional addresses and daily expositions of Scripture.

We sailed from Plymouth Sound for Hobart Town, Tasmania, on Oct. 5th, and had proceeded but a short way on our voyage, when I received a letter from one of the prisoners, in which, after expressing his views of himself as a sinner and a convict, he proceeds to lament the injury he had inflicted on his country, the disgrace he had brought upon his relatives and friends, and, above all, that he had so offended and grieved that blessed Saviour who had suffered and died upon the cross, that he, a guilty transgressor, might not perish, but have everlasting life. He goes on, with much apparent honesty of feeling, to speak of the number and aggravation of his sins, of the punishment which he deserves, and also of the encouragement with which he sometimes thinks on the Saviour's lovingkindness and forbearance. In alluding to his crimes, he particularizes those of drunkenness, profane swearing, and lying; and admits that his guilt is vastly increased by his privileges having exceeded those of many in his station in life, as he had been sent to school, taught to read, and had even received instruction at a sabbath-school; and I may observe that he was one of the *very few* convicts who I ever ascertained had attended such an institution. After noticing the kindness of his sabbath-school teachers, he makes the most touching allusions to his mother, and dwells on a *mother's* kind affection,—a *mother's* "walk in the ways of godliness,"—a *mother's* prayers poured out "over" him at her bedside in secret,—a *mother's* faithful and beseeching advice rejected by her wayward son—a *mother's broken heart!*—"I was the cause," says he, "of breaking her heart;"—it was broken "through my disobedience!"—"But, blessed be God, she is in glory now!—She was so familiar with death, she was prepared to die at any moment. She died in my absence, and knew not where I was, nor how I was getting on. What has God done for me, a hell-deserving convict!" He mentions the influence which a treatise on the "barren fig-tree" had produced upon his mind since he came on board, and the insight it had given him into his own character; and then alludes to some of the great and precious promises of the gospel; those especially in Matt. xi., the chapter we had read in our usual course the preceding evening. He makes also grateful reference to the first chapter of Isaiah. His interesting and really affecting letter concludes with thankful, and even joyous reference to the marvellous dispensations of the providence of God in bringing about his embarkation in the *Earl Grey*, where provision was made for the spiritual instruction of himself and the other "poor ignorant convicts;"—and expresses an earnest desire for his own growth in grace, and the success of our labours among his fellow-prisoners.

Any appearance of improvement in a convict, we are disposed to view with suspicion. In every thing relating to their reformation, we are apt to set limits to the Holy One of Israel. But while we regard with prudent caution and circumspection all mere professions of repentance and change of views, we must attach a just degree of weight to evident and unquestionable improvement in temper and conduct. To doubt the power of God to convert by his Spirit a convict, through the knowledge of Jesus Christ his Son, is to dishonour God, to deny the sovereignty and omnipotence of his grace, and to place ourselves, who are made to differ only by the same grace, beyond the reach of his gospel, and of the consistent exercise of his mercy. The letter, just referred to, I received with thankfulness to the Father of mercies, not only as it regarded the writer himself, but as "a token for good," respecting the people, among whom I hoped a work of grace was begun. I may add, that, in private conversations with this man, for the purpose of giving him suitable counsel, he evinced such knowledge of the plague of his own heart, soundness of views concerning salvation, and apparent thirst for Christ and the sanctifying influence of His truth, as warranted the conclusion that he was *taught of God.*

From another prisoner I had previously received a written communication calculated to awaken hope; and there were many whose entire carriage and conduct comported with the knowledge and love of Divine truth,—although they had not yet, in words, declared themselves "on the Lord's side." The foregoing pages will show that the whole of the prisoners were in abiding and immediate contact with the gospel of Christ,—were ever, so to speak, moving in the Divine presence, which is promised to accompany the reading of His word, scriptural exhortation, and prayer; but though we are thus warranted to look for the Divine blessing, yet we may be required to wait long in the exercise of believing patience.

A THUNDER STORM. 55

About two o'clock on the morning of the 2d of November, and when nearly in 9° north latitude, and 21° west longitude, the thermometer ranging from 82° to 83°, and the barometer as high as thirty inches, I was suddenly roused from sleep by the most rending peals of thunder, the most vivid flashes of lightning, and in an instant I sprang from my bed, and stood upon the deck. I was then suffering from a violent affection of the heart, and was unable to leave my cabin; but if I had been able, it was, at that moment, the most suitable place for me. My presence elsewhere could have proved of no advantage to any one. The hour was one in which all were as from heaven called to the footstool of the throne of mercy and grace,— even those whose duty required them to be either actively or passively engaged in works of necessity and mercy, were called to lift up, in the faith of Jesus, their hearts unto God.

No language can possibly describe the scene in the midst of which I then stood, and by which I saw and felt myself encompassed. All creation seemed on fire. Thunder, the loudest that ever fell upon my ear, prevailed in every quarter;—peal upon peal followed in rapid succession;—the distant roar contrasted with that in which I felt myself enwrapped, and the one or the other never ceased:—sometimes several peals, either close to us, or at various distances from us, prevailed together. The lightning's flash was too vivid for the eyes to look upon, and, both near and at a distance, scarcely allowed a moment's intermission. The thick Egyptian darkness which intervened was but for a moment; but even that moment gave to the senses and the mind no repose,—it was darkness that was terrific in itself, and gave to the winged thunderbolts and the electric corruscations that covered the face of the heavens, a more piercing glare—a more overpowering vividness. The rain fell in torrents,—the breath of heaven had died away,—all things appeared to listen in awe to the voice of the Eternal, and to watch the manifestation and direction of His power. The ship was alone on the face of the wild ocean, and in the midst of threatening and destructive elements; Creation appeared to be breaking up,—all things were full of the Divine power: the angry elements testified to the guilty the Divine displeasure, and powerfully suggested "the coming of the day of God, wherein the heavens being on fire shall be dissolved, and the elements shall melt with fervent heat." The soul—the conscience, was confronted with God:—and the truths of reason, and the inspired truths of revelation, written on the tablets of the heart by the Holy Ghost, were read by the awakened spirit in the light of living fire! The voice of God, heard in the thunder of His power, was heard also in the awful sanctions of His holy law, and in the immutable requirements of a neglected gospel. The scene was well fitted to carry us to the foot of that mount which, in the sight of Israel's hosts, was covered with the thick cloud—was encompassed with thunders and lightnings, from the midst of which proceeded the sound of the trumpet, waxing louder and louder, and the voice of God, when He had descended in fire, to deliver to man that holy law which

announces naught but death to the transgressor; whose guilty mind can know no true and lasting peace, until he find it on Calvary, under the sprinkling of the atoning blood of the Divine Lawgiver Himself—our blessed Emanuel, on the accursed tree slain for us!*
The hour—the very hour of death, was felt at hand—the moment of the soul's unclothing† and appearance in the immediate presence of the Judge,—to be seen in its true character,—in the character *then* worked out,—to be dealt with in perfect accordance with that character by God Himself in the midst of the seen and felt realities of the eternal world,—free from all guise,—stripped of all pretence,—disrobed of all garments of human texture,—to be fixed,—for ever fixed,—according to the choice made in life,—made in the body,—unalterably fixed for ceaseless ages, in *sorrow* or in *joy*,—according as Christ shall have been, in life, accepted or put away,—according as the Holy Spirit shall have been, in life, received to renewal unto holiness, or criminally resisted, and pollution and death preferred. Oh, what is man,—what is sinful and guilty man, when viewed in the light of God's fiery law,—of the Divine perfections,—the all-pervading light of Omniscience,—and surrounded with all the realities of the eternal world? When we feel ourselves encompassed with the Divine presence, and experience the fiery consciousness of His perfect knowledge of us, or of our utter vileness in his sight,—when the soul is about to quit its clay tenement, to be removed from the sound of the Gospel for ever! and to have its

---

* Exod. xix. xx.; Heb. xii.   † 2 Cor. v.

own chosen state for ever fixed,—what then can avail us any thing but *a personal,—a saving interest in Christ?* What can give peace to the conscience, and cover all our iniquities, but His precious blood, shed upon the cross as a sacrifice for sin, and effectually applied to our souls, through faith, by the power of the Holy Ghost? What can secure us from shame before Him at His coming, and inspire us with holy and child-like confidence when he appeareth, but the anointing* of the Holy Spirit of promise setting His seal upon us,† and bearing witness with our spirits that we are the children of God‡ by faith in Christ Jesus? What then sustains and comforts the mind in reference to our beloved relatives and friends, but scriptural evidence that they have fled for refuge to lay hold upon the hope set before them in the gospel, and have become the subjects of a heavenly birth? And, oh, how awful—how absolutely insupportable, the conviction then, that we—now about to die,— have *neglected* them—have not been faithful to them concerning their souls—have not with all our might, by consistent example, and in the power of prayer in the Holy Ghost, urged them to flee to Jesus, to flee at once, and in Him take refuge from the wrath to come! Oh, how true it is that dying moments should have nothing left for them to do but the work of dying!—of dying in peace, to the glory of our Redeemer, and to the benefit of souls,—dying in the confidence of Him in whom we have believed, and still do

---

* 1 John ii. 20, 27—29. † Ephesians iv. 30.
‡ Romans viii. 16. Read these three chapters.

believe; whom we have loved, and still do love; whose service we have felt to be our perfect freedom,—in whose presence we have experienced joy,—and hope to experience fulness of joy; and at whose right-hand, through free and sovereign grace, we have the well-grounded hope of enjoying pleasures for evermore!

The storm continued to rage, in all the terribleness of its fury. No human voice was heard, save the voice, and that but rarely, of the officer carrying on duty. The mind was kept in solemn and awful watchfulness: the annihilation of the ship, the destruction of all on board, seemed at hand; we lay on the borders of eternity! At length a body of electric fire, commonly called a "thunder-bolt," struck the fore-royal mast, shivered it into pieces, melted the copper in the sheave-hole, passed down the masts and the iron chain halliards, and having partially diffused itself through the parts of the vessel immediately adjoining the combings of the foremast, struck, though not fatally, three men: after doing various damage, it entered the prison, passed round the decks amongst the prisoners, and then disappeared. For some time, until the carpenter sounded the well, it was doubtful whether or not the ship was about to go down, and for awhile she seemed on fire. I stood watching with my feet the indications of the deck, whether the vessel was sinking or not, and with breathless solicitude listened for the prisoners' shriek when they should feel the water rising upon them, and the ship descending into the deep, to be buried with all on board, under the waves. The scene now appeared to have reached its climax of awful impressiveness. The manifestations of Omnipotence were now unutterably overwhelming to the mind, the realities of the unseen world now threatened to open on our view, and to appear before us in the light of the fire of God's own kindling.

The prison, as testified by two hundred and sixty-four men, exhibited a scene that no language can describe. The prisoners were laid prostrate; most, if not all of them stretched on the deck,—every object seemed lighted up with electric fire!—the broad-headed iron nails with which the bars placed around the hatchways are studded, were almost brilliantly illuminated, and appeared as if consuming. The prisoners lay along under their burdens of sin and guilt,—their past lives were placed before them in more than the light of the fierce thunder-bolts, for they had by this time been instructed in the Scriptures, they had all in some degree learned the requirements, and the penalties of God's "holy law"—they had all heard of His love,— of the unspeakable gift of His love, of His revealed "long-suffering, and unwillingness that any should perish, but that all should come to repentance;"* all had heard of the Divine efficacy of the blood of Christ to wash away all sin, and speak peace to the guiltiest conscience; and they had heard the invitation and command of God that they should believe on the name of His Son Jesus Christ for present and everlasting life, and love one another as He gave us commandment.†
They thought that the hour of final account, the great

---

* 2 Peter iii. 9.   † 1 John iii. 23.

day of judgment was come, at least that to *them* time should be no longer, and that their eternal state would now in a few moments be for ever fixed! They already felt that God was dealing with them as his responsible creatures, and with solemn, perplexing, and unquiet anxiety were they now compelled to deal with themselves, and that in the midst of the most fearful tokens of the Almighty power and all-searching knowledge of that holy, merciful, and just God whom they had despised, and whose beloved Son, together with His great salvation, they had wickedly put away. The things of time they now saw in all their unsatisfying vanity, and felt the paramount importance of an interest in the friendship of Him who alone is the efficient friend of sinners,—who laid down His life to redeem them, and who alone "is able to save to the uttermost all who come unto God by Him, seeing that he only ever liveth to make intercession for them."

All that passed at this time through the minds of the prisoners, all the communication which took place between them and God, is known only to Him who searcheth the heart and tries the reins of the children of men.

After a period of about two hours, the flashes gradually became less vivid, the thunder more distant; all was ultimately hushed into serenity and peace, and the mind was left to its thoughts, to make a suitable improvement of God's fearful yet merciful visit, and lay to heart all the solemn lessons which He ever intends to teach, when He thus passes by in the whirlwind, the earthquake or the fire.

On the following morning, when I visited the prison, deep seriousness seemed to pervade every mind. All the prisoners appeared to have been deeply affected, and all were disposed to dwell upon the scene they had witnessed, and to make it the subject of solemn conversation. We assembled below for reading the Scriptures, and prayer; and in addition to our proper chapter for the morning, which was Matthew xviii., we read Job xxxvi. and xxxvii.; and endeavoured, in a solemn address to the people, to make a suitable and practical improvement of the previous night's dispensation, and of God's marvellous manifestation of long suffering and sparing mercy. In the evening, we again made seasonable allusion to the momentous and impressive subject. With several of the people I conversed in private on the things belonging to their peace, and with much satisfaction. The instructions received from the Bible seemed to have been much more deeply impressed on the heart than I had hitherto imagined. To understand Christianity had from the day of their embarkation been their great business, and with one accord they now seemed to feel that it was a business of which they ought not to be ashamed, and their attachment to which it was consistent to avow,—sinful and unsafe to conceal. The manifestation of the Divine power, and intimations of a coming judgment, had rendered it, in their view, quite reasonable that the everlasting concerns of the immortal soul, together with the glory of God, should be made the great business of life. The melancholy intelligence received from the ship *Duchess of Northumberland*, with which we communicated shortly after the thunder-storm, of the wreck of the convict ship *Waterloo* at the Cape of Good Hope, and the consequent loss of *one hundred and eighty* prisoners, and *fifteen* soldiers, made a deep impression upon all our minds, and afforded subject of touching address and admonition to the people in the *Earl Grey*.

From this time our occasional addresses and daily expositions of sacred Scriptures became more pointed and personal, our dealings with the conscience more close and pressing. The gospel was now exhibited in its most encouraging aspect to the most depraved and unworthy among depraved and despised convicts; —redemption was more closely and impressively set forth in its relation to the fixed and immutable principles of the moral government of the universe; close, personal and regular examinations of the people on their acquaintance with Scripture, and particularly with reference to their views of the way of salvation, were commenced, and proved most interesting and instructive to the people, all of whom were, on these and all other occasions of meeting for devotional exercises, assembled and closely seated together, either in the prison, or on the upper deck. The application of the prisoners to their Bibles and other good books, and the manliness and correctness of their behaviour, were most remarkable and pleasing. Private conversations with those who desired to converse with me respecting their personal salvation, became more frequent. *Seven* of my men I felt warranted to regard as being taught of God; and shortly after *four* were added to their number.

By the 7th of December, to my joyous satisfaction, I was able to regard *eleven* of my prisoners as disposed by God's grace to submit to the authority of Christ, to take up His cross and follow Him. On the following day, these *eleven men* met in the widest part of the prison, in which our daily worship was conducted when the weather prevented our being on the upper deck; and in the presence of all the people, after prayer to God, they were solemnly addressed as men who professed, through grace, to bewail the plague of their own hearts, the wickedness of their past lives, their lawless conduct and evil example, to feel their desert of everlasting condemnation, and need of Divine deliverance;—as men who, by the teaching of God's word and Spirit, had, through His infinite mercy, been led to perceive the all-sufficiency of the obedience and death of Christ to give peace and acceptance with God and to save the chief of sinners; as men who had obeyed the command of God to believe on His Son Jesus Christ, and desired henceforth to be the Lord's —to live to His honour and glory, to cast in their lot with His people,—and thankfully to submit to the promised teaching of the Holy Spirit, to qualify them for all the duties of life, and prepare them for the glory and the rest of heaven!

Thus were these *eleven* men voluntarily formed into a Christian society for the worship of God, and observance, as far as present circumstances allowed, of His appointed ordinances; for mutual edification and comfort, and exhibition of the light of Divine truth to the prisoners around them.

To the Lord we looked up in prayer and faith for direction in the selection of a suitable portion of Scripture for this solemn and most affecting occasion, and were unexpectedly led to Paul's epistle to Philemon, which furnished the most impressive and encouraging instruction to us all, particularly that portion of it which more immediately relates to the history and conversion of Onesimus, a servant or slave, who had unlawfully absconded from his master, after having, as some think, robbed him. In the all-wise and gracious arrangements of Divine Providence, he had been led to Rome, where, through the preaching of the Apostle Paul, he was brought to the saving knowledge of Christ, of which he gave immediate evidence by his affectionate attendance, as a Christian *"son,"* on that spiritual father, through whose means, by the power of the Lord, this criminal runaway had been begotten again to a lively hope. The Apostle, much to his inconvenience, sends him back to his master, requesting that he may be received, not now as a servant or slave, but as a " brother beloved," even as Paul himself; and in the true spirit of Christianity generously charges his friend Philemon, "If he hath wronged thee, or oweth thee aught, put that on mine account: I, Paul, have written it with mine own hand, I will repay it."

The case of Onesimus admitted of the most happy and encouraging application to that of the prisoners. Without interfering with their responsibility, the holy providence of God was overruling their wickedness for good:—they, like Onesimus, were brought under the preaching of the gospel even in a prison; like him they were shown by the Holy Spirit, from the inspired writings of the same Apostle, that the blood of Jesus Christ cleanseth from all sin, and that now they are, by God, commanded to repent and believe the gospel, and obtain, as the free gift of the Most High, without money and without price, the forgiveness of all their sins, the renovation of their nature, the new heart and the right spirit; to be "no more strangers and foreigners, but fellow-citizens with the saints, and of the household of *God*,"—to be, each of them, like Onesimus, "*a brother beloved*," to the praise of the unsearchable riches of Christ! Although our meeting was special and peculiar, our exercises, as usual, consisted in prayer, reading of the Scriptures, exposition, exhortation, praise, and thanksgiving; the psalms and hymns being selected for the occasion. Before the address was delivered, the names of the professing disciples of the Lord Jesus were distinctly announced in the hearing of all present. The meeting was most solemn and affecting. The visible *obedience* of these *eleven* men, in thus confessing the name of their blessed Lord and Saviour before their fellow-prisoners, and not forsaking the assembling of themselves together, as the manner of some is, made a strong impression on the minds of observers.*

Their confession of the faith of Jesus was made not only in the presence of men, but of angels; and *God* himself was witness!—witness of the state of our hearts, the agreement of which, with that which the human

---

* Matt. x. 32—39; Heb. x. 19—25.

eye beheld, He alone could see, who will continue to witness the agreement or disagreement of our entire succeeding life and conduct, with the solemn and public profession we made on the eighth day of December, 1842; and where shall we find power to walk in peace and holiness, but in the influence of the Holy Spirit, and in continual dependence on the precious blood of Jesus?

The complexion of our meetings for Divine worship was, from henceforth, changed. Besides the congregation, consisting of all the other prisoners, there were the professing disciples, who, through grace, had by faith and holy obedience been separated from the rest,*—who now desired to follow Christ, through evil report and good report, according to His word,—and who, feeling that they had *"much forgiven"* them, were under the highest obligation to *"love much,"* and henceforth to dedicate themselves, body, soul, and spirit, to Him who redeemed them to Himself by His blood.

A prisoner named *George Day*, who had for some time been ill, was confined to his bed, which happened to be near the place where I was standing when speaking from the Epistle to Philemon. He was not in my sight, for a number of the people were seated in front of his berth, but I afterwards learned that he had listened most earnestly and anxiously to all that was said. And when he heard of Onesimus's charac-

---

*Acts v. 12—14; xix. 9; 2 Thess. iii. 6—16; 1 Tim. vi. 1—5; Rom. xvi. 17; 2 Tim iii. 1—5; Eph v. 11.

ter and conversion, he exclaimed to the following effect, unheard, as he thought, by any around him: "What! a runaway slave, that had robbed his master! —he converted!—he brought to Christ!—he received back and pardoned!—he saved!—a runaway slave saved!—and why not a convict?" breathed out the soul of poor George Day;—"why not a poor wretched convict? Will not Jesus receive *me* too? Is not His blood able to wash away all *my* sins?—May not *I* be saved?" And in this state of mind be continued; sometimes filled with joy, sometimes with anxiety and fear. He passed almost a sleepless night. His mind could not now rest until he knew that his soul was safe, and that he had obtained an interest in Christ; for as yet he had obtained no settled peace. But he was perplexed by the inquiry, "*When* am I to obtain the salvation of my soul? *when* may I expect to be put in possession of the salvation in which Onesimus rejoiced?" In this state of anxious perplexity, and longing for deliverance, he continued, almost constantly in prayer, until the following evening, when we assembled for our usual devotions, John v. happened to be our appointed portion for that evening, and I was led to dwell on the urgent practical application of the 24th verse, viewed in connexion with John iii. 36. To all that was said, George Day, whilst lying in his bed, was listening with the most eager attention and devout appropriation. But he shall speak for himself, in the following brief and somewhat unconnected statement, which I received some time after he had openly confessed the name of

Jesus. It was dictated by himself, when still confined to bed, and suffering severely from old and confirmed disease, and was written from his lips on a slip of paper, by a fellow-prisoner, who afterwards gave it to me:*

* * * "I bless and praise the Lord that ever I came on board this vessel; for here the Lord has had mercy upon me, and brought me to feel myself a guilty sinner in His sight. I have been greatly afflicted; but I hope my afflictions have been greatly blessed to my soul. I, for many years, have been living in the service of the devil. I was what might be termed a travelling thief, and remained hardened, though arrested for my crimes, imprisoned, and now transported,—until I came on board the *Earl Grey*, bound to Hobart Town. Blessed be God, the kind instruction from God's holy word has been the means of my soul's salvation. I was very ill, but remained quite unconcerned until I heard the Epistle to Philemon read. I was then led to compare my last life with the life of Onesimus, the runaway servant, who found pardon and became a new man; and it powerfully came to my mind, that the same Saviour could and would save even me, if I came to Him by faith and repentance. I hope I *prayed*, but found but little peace until I heard the doctor pressing upon our at-

---

* The preceding account was written from the report I received at the time. This statement was written shortly before the debarkation took place; I transcribe it, with the alteration of only one word, which correctness required.

tention the words of God, contained in the 3d chapter of John, verse 36, and 5th chapter, verse 24. I could scarcely believe it to be true at the time; for it seemed as though a *voice* spoke to me, '*He that believeth in the Son hath everlasting life!*' I was *astonished!* I sprang up in my bed,—I said to myself, '*Hath* everlasting life!' What! *me*, Lord? so unholy! so unworthy! *Hath* it!—*Hath* it!—Can it be so? Blessed be the Lord, I found the promise true,—I believed; I cast myself at the feet of Jesus; I found mercy. I can rejoice in the Lord Jesus; I have no hope but in Him. I am very ill still; but, I trust though my illness is painful at present, it will soon terminate in the Lord's way; either I shall go to inherit life everlasting, or shall live supported by my Lord, who is my life, my joy, my trust, my everlasting All. His will be done! If I live, may I live to the Lord: if I die, may I die unto the Lord! Oh, may I meet my Benefactor in heaven,—with my dear fellow-prisoners who have believed through Divine grace! Glory to the Lord for what He has done for so many of us! May He keep us through all the trials we may have to pass through in our sad situation as prisoners; may we be kept from sin, and be helped to let 'our light so shine before men, that others seeing our good works may glorify our Father who is in heaven.'—Amen."

This man was born in the army; and having learned no trade, entered, in process of time, on a very irregular course of life. Unhappily, too, for himself, as it respected both soul and body, he was for some time engaged in the service of the Queen of Spain. He was a great invalid during fully the last half of our voyage, and on arrival at *Hobart,* he was sent to the Colonial Hospital; in which a truly pious, judicious, and zealous medical officer* of the army officiated, whose Christian interest in his patients, and unwearied labours for their temporal and spiritual good, indicated the power of the gospel on his own heart, and through the Divine blessing, could not fail to prove most soothing and beneficial to those who were placed under his care. In this hospital, as soon as my health permitted, I visited Day, and ever found him in the most blessed frame of mind, though in the midst of great affliction. He appeared never for a moment to have lost his confidence in the Saviour,—and his rejoicing in His finished redemption was ever accompanied with the deepest humility, self-abasement and self-distrust. His feet seemed fixed on the Rock of Ages; his joy was in the freeness and the riches of Divine grace; his consolations were evidently the promised consolations of the Holy Spirit. Some time before I left the colony he *died*—and died, there are the best reasons for believing, holding fast *Christ,* the beginning of his confidence, and the rejoicing of his hope, steadfastly even unto the end.†

The paper containing the foregoing statement of George Day, was accompanied with a short note from

---

* Dr. Mair, Staff Surgeon. † Heb. iii.

the prisoner who transmitted it to me, from which I make the following brief quotation, in order to show, in some degree, the writer's state of mind, with reference to himself and the other prisoners:

* * * "Please to allow me, in behalf of the great body of my poor dear fellow-sufferers,—especially those to whom the cross of Jesus has been made the power of God unto salvation, and to whom the Word of the Lord is precious and consoling, to thank you with all our hearts, and the kind people to England, for their pity and aid in supplying us so richly with those blessed words of God." * * *

This note anticipates in a measure our report of the gracious work of the Holy Spirit in the hearts of an increasing number of our prisoners. Day after day saw another and another of the men apparently "*plucked*" by the hand of Sovereign mercy, as "*a brand out of the fire*,"* and added to the number of the monuments of rich and free grace in Christ Jesus, adorning the gospel by consistent conduct, unceasing and earnest prayer, and by active and well-directed zeal, for the spiritual instruction and salvation of all around them.

On the night of Dec. 13th, about ten o'clock, a heavy sea fell aboard the *Earl Grey*, and a great body of water poured through the main and after-hatchways into the hospital and prison. I was at the time engaged in abstracting blood from the arm of a prisoner suffering under a severe inflammatory affec-

* Zech. iii. 2.

tion, and could not well make my escape from the torrents. To the minds of most of the prisoners the scene was terrific. Nearly all of them were asleep at the time the sea fell on the deck, and awoke up in a state of great alarm; and their agitation continued for some time, through the fearful noise made by the water flowing down the hatchways, washing from side to side by the rolling of the ship, and carrying with it every thing that had not been securely fixed, dashing it against the sides of the prison. To get rid of my wet clothes and prepare for attending properly on my patient, I was carried through the water to the prison-door on the back of one of my men. A considerable time elapsed before the water obtained an exit from our decks. The men who occupied the lower range of berths, particularly in the after-part of the prison, fled, and took refuge for the night in those above them, leaving their wet bedding to be dried, if possible, during the ensuing day. The person and bedding of one poor man, named John Williams, who was at the time suffering from consumption of the lungs, were so wet that a cold chill came on, the effects of which bade defiance to all remedies, and on the morning of the 15th he *died*. The scene of the night of the 13th, the death of Williams two days after,—his funeral—the portions of Scripture read, and the address delivered on the occasion, made a strong and deep impression on the minds of many of the prisoners, and seemed more or less to affect them all, leading many of them to *God*, through the power of the Holy Spirit, by the faith and obedience of the gospel.

Poor Williams, up to a short period before his death, gave no *satisfactory* evidence of change of heart. During the last few days of his life he exhibited some promising symptoms of contrition and repentance, and during the twenty-four hours immediately preceding his death, he ceased not to acknowledge that he was a most guilty and helpless sinner, referred to the Lord Jesus as the only object of his trust, and *seemed* to cast himself humbly and devoutly on his pardoning mercy. But here we must, in awful and most painful uncertainty, leave him. Of a death-bed repentance we are scarcely authorized to speak, except when it is accompanied with some very special circumstances, some strong and decided manifestation of the power of the Holy Spirit,—some clear and distinctive marks of his Divine and saving teaching. The Bible encourages no man to delay, for a single moment, his reception of Christ, when once set before him in the proclamation of the gospel; which is ever accompanied with the command of God, that every one who hears it do *immediately* believe it, for pardon, purification, and life. It is most true, that whosoever, even in the last moment of life, believeth in the Son of God, *hath* everlasting life, and shall not come into condemnation, but *is* passed from death unto life. But man can know nothing of the change of the heart but by the fruits of the life. When circumstances admit not of the production of the unquestionable fruits of righteousness, then circumstances allow not man to form a judgment. The Lord looketh upon the heart; He knows its state and all its exercises; and if He should be graciously pleased to give, at the eleventh hour, a living faith in Jesus, He will save the soul on which He hath, in his abundant and long-suffering mercy, conferred such a gift. But when life is not prolonged, to afford opportunity of manifesting that faith in holy and consistent obedience, we cannot look beyond the veil which is spread before our view. All that the Bible affirms is true, and will most assuredly be accomplished; every divine promise will be fulfilled to the believer in Jesus; but it is an awful sin, involving the most fearful danger, for any man to *delay* his believing reception of Christ and of the Holy Spirit, and the production of those fruits of holiness which prove the possession of that faith which overcomes the world, and works by love; and of that blessed hope which leads its possessor to purify himself even as Christ is pure.

One prisoner from amongst the first seven who appeared to have received the truth in the love of it, and to take up the cross to follow Christ, was named J—— V——.

This man, I found, at the time our schools were organized, so well educated that I appointed him one of my teachers. But I was not aware of the destructive principles he had imbibed, or the pernicious habits he had formed, otherwise I should not have placed him in such an important and responsible situation. His appearance and general deportment being rather pleasing, his scholarship and willingness to teach, induced me to select him, with others, for the important office of teaching the people to read the Bible—never dreaming that he was prepared to avail himself of that position to substitute for food the most destructive poison, and to pervert the opportunity offered to him of serving God, into an opportunity of promoting the work of Satan, by seducing souls to licentiousness, infidelity, and death? Of his principles and character I heard nothing, until I learnt that he was under anxious concern for his soul. The following confession of his principles and life, made soon after he was brought under the influence of the gospel, and written down from his own lips, by a fellow-prisoner, will best set forth the fearful danger to which he was exposed, and from which his complete rescue could be effected by nothing short of the almighty power of the Word and Spirit of God:

"J—— V—— desires with all his heart and soul to bless the Lord for bringing him on board the *Earl Grey*." He says, "I came on board what I had been for a long time, in my principles, a *confirmed Socialist*. Having embraced *Owen's* doctrines, I took every opportunity of instilling them into the minds of others. I made an attack upon one of the schoolmasters on board, and concluded, after a long tussle with him,— even with the Bible in hand,—that I had gained a most decisive victory. This encouraged me to do all the mischief I could, by bringing my fellow-prisoners to my faith: and it is a mercy indeed that I was stopt in my mad career; or the mischief I would have done might have been great. In the way I have mentioned I went on until the night of November 2d, when the thunder-bolt came upon us. I was *terrified*, —my principles did not support my mind; but in the morning I attempted to laugh it off, and called myself a *fool* for being so fearful. But at the time of prayer, we were spoken to in a very kind, but faithful manner, and warned to flee from the wrath to come—unto Jesus, the only security and peace of a perishing sinner.

"One Scripture was repeated which went like a dagger to my heart, namely this, 'O Jerusalem, Jerusalem, thou that killest the prophets, and stonest them which are sent unto thee, how often would I have gathered thy children together, even as a hen gathereth her chickens under her wings, and ye would not.'* '*Ye would not,*' struck upon my heart all day long. I remembered how God had been calling to me by many providences,—and still 'I *would not.*' The Lord Jesus seemed to say to me from the cross, '*Why will you not come to Me?*'—I could get no rest. I was horrified by my wickedness, and the abominable system I had embraced, and could not indulge a hope of mercy. But the Lord sent the same word time after time to my mind, and every time with more power —'*Why will you not come to Me?*'—Thank the Lord! —after some days I found my mind *humbling*, and felt a stronger desire to know Jesus, whom I persecuted. I prayed as well as I could; and He, at length, did bring me to cast myself down, as it were, at his feet, and cry out, 'Lord, save me, a guilty sinner!' I had for some time *only a hope*—and that very faint; but He soon lifted up upon me the light of His recon-

---

* Matt. xxiii. 37.

ciled countenance; and that brought peace to my mind, which I shall enjoy. And my earnest prayer is, that I may spend the remnant of my days as a true and humble follower of Jesus."

Such is the confession,—such a brief view of, I trust, the conversion of a *Socialist*. His spirit and conduct, from this time, were unexceptionable in every respect. Not the breath of a complaint affecting him ever reached me, or any of my petty officers or schoolmasters. As a teacher, he was most useful, and most exemplary. He became a diligent student of the Bible, and of other useful and devotional books. He appeared to grow in grace as well as in knowledge: his prayers evinced his acquaintance with the doctrines of redemption and an experimental knowledge of his own spiritual wants and necessities. He now laboured more strenuously to cast down the kingdom of Satan than ever he had laboured to build it up, and was more zealous and unwearied in promoting the reign of Jesus in the hearts of his fellow-sinners, than he had ever been in opposing it.

Should this brief statement meet the eye of any one unhappily entangled by the debasing and destructive principles and practices of Socialism, we would pray and hope that it may arrest his attention,—lead him to reflect seriously on the fearful tendency of that pernicious system in which he has involved himself,— dispose him to commence, without a moment's delay, the devout, candid, and diligent study of the writings of inspiration, the *sixty-six* sacred books, which God has graciously given to us as the only rule of our *be-*

lief, our *practice*, and our *hope;* and if he begin and continue his inquiries in a teachable and child-like, or, if he please, in a *truly manly* spirit, with an honest desire to know the will of God, manifesting itself in a ready, and cheerful performance of *that will*, at whatever cost, the moment it is ascertained,—and if he look up to the Father, through Jesus Christ, for the promised gift of the Holy Spirit, and rely wholly on His teaching and guidance, he will assuredly be rescued from the entanglements, pollution, guilt, and wretchedness of Socialism, from the power of sin and Satan, and be found, like the maniac of old, sitting at the feet of Jesus, his gracious Deliverer—clothed, and in his right mind, enjoying that blessed and holy liberty wherewith He makes all His people free; and prepared to spend the remainder of his days in the service of God, a blessing to his country, and wise in winning souls to Christ, who will preserve him and them in the faith and obedience of the gospel, even unto His everlasting kingdom and glory!

CHAPTER IV.

Account of W. B.—Special prayers—Converts increase—F. M.—J. S.

Among the prisoners who embarked at Woolwich was one named W—— B——, about *thirty* years of age, a man, as it afterwards appeared, of a delicate constitution, and subject to a variety of bodily ailments. When proceeding down the English Channel, he was taken ill, and confined to his bed. Having inquired into his case, I did not consider him a fit subject for a long voyage in a crowded ship, and resolved to apply for his debarkation on our arrival at Plymouth. When charged with acting in neglect, if not in defiance, of the advice which I had positively given to the whole of the prisoners on board the hulks, he assured me, from his knowledge of his constitution, that a milder climate would prove very advantageous to his health, and that he hoped soon to get well, and make himself useful to me in any way I might think fit to employ him. I was still determined, however, according to the spirit of my instructions, to have him sent on shore, apprehensive that the voyage might prove hazardous to his life. On the following morning he sent me a note, in which he *implored* me to allow him to remain in the *Earl Grey;* and a further investigation of his case ultimately satisfied me that I might, with propriety, *permit* him to proceed on the voyage. By the time we reached the latitude of Madeira, his health improved; he became one of my most useful teachers; and gave, in process of time, the most satisfactory and pleasing evidence that he was a true child of God by faith in Christ Jesus. He evinced talents of rather a superior order, had been pretty well educated, exhibited great manliness of deportment, and possessed a most remarkably sound judgment, great discernment of character, and considerable acquaintance with Scripture, and the peculiar doctrines of the gospel. His personal piety seemed deep, influential, and abiding; his interest in the salvation of the souls around him ardent and practical. After he had been about two months on board, he never ceased to care for his fellow-prisoners, and was always ready to attend to my instructions, and aid me in every possible way. When our voyage was well advanced, I requested him to give me in writing a few particulars of his past life, and received the following statement:

* * * * * " It is with great sorrow of mind I write, when I reflect upon the errors and wickedness of my past life; but also, I trust, with great love and gratitude to God, when I take, as I now do, a retrospective view of the undeserved mercy of my Creator and Redeemer towards me. If my heart is not deceiving me, I can unite sincerely with David, saying, 'Bless the Lord, O my soul, and all that is within me, bless His Holy name, and forget not all His benefits.'

"I was born December 27th, 1812, in London. I was

not favoured with God-fearing parents, and was brought up in sin, until I arrived at the age of twelve years, when my father, who had carried on a respectable and rather extensive trade, became embarrassed through a variety of trials and losses in trade, which broke his spirits, and he soon became the tenant of the tomb,—dying, I fear, without an interest in Jesus Christ. My mother was left in trouble, but the Lord graciously raised up kind friends. A change of circumstances, however, caused her to leave her hitherto comfortable home, and to labour for her maintenance in the service of a private gentleman. My lot was to be sent into the country, my dear grandfather taking charge of me. The Lord, I trust, when I was at the Sabath-school, in the village of S—— N——, first led me to see my ruined state by nature, and, I hope, notwithstanding my subsequent shameful and painful departure from the way of peace, that, at the age of thirteen years, I was, in rich mercy, brought to a saving knowledge of the Lord Jesus. Oh, how sweet the memory of the peaceful and happy hours I then spent in walking humbly with the Lord,—and in sweet communion with him! With pain of mind I must tell you, I became united with God's people; I do not grieve that I joined the Christian Society, but that by my wickedness I have disgraced my profession, wounded the holy and blessed Saviour, who had done so much for my soul, grieved the Holy Spirit, and brought the Lord's dear people into affliction. Oh, what evil have I done! Oh, that my repentance may prove to be that which is unto life, and which shall never need to be repented of!

"But to proceed. I remember when my teacher was, one sabbath, contrasting the happiness of the believer with the misery of the wicked, I thought of my dear departed father, who, I feared, could not go to heaven as he died. This led me, through the Holy Spirit's teaching, to consider the state of my own soul; and I hope the work of grace then commenced in my heart. (I was about *thirteen* years of age.) From the age of *sixteen*, when I became a member of a Christian Church, up to my *twenty-second* year, I continued at S——, and was engaged in the Sabbath-school, and in various other efforts with God's people, to advance his glory. During that time, I, to the praise of the Lord, can say that I was truly enabled to adorn the doctrine of God our Saviour, and to walk as becometh the gospel. At the age of *twenty-two*, I came to London; and being in bad health, and my trade laborious, my friends obtained for me a situation in a tradesman's office. For three years I was enabled to maintain a character consistent with the Christian profession; and being anxious to get on in life, I applied myself diligently to my master's interests, and was, at the end of that time, made his town-traveller, and succeeded in my efforts to increase his connexion. But my new sphere of business brought me into more frequent intercourse with worldly minds; and being exposed, as a matter of course, to the temptation of drinking with my customers, in time—to my shame and sorrow—that which I had *disliked*, namely, ardent spirits, I became fond of. Many struggles, sharp and distressing, passed in my poor disordered mind between the powers of grace and sin; but, alas! it became a confirmed habit with me to drink, and to mingle with some who, though respectable in society, proved enemies to my poor soul. Several of these were my best customers, and my anxiety to increase trade through them brought me at first into contact with them, and led me to court their society, which ultimately accelerated my sad and awful fall.

"But the great evil, and that which lay at the foundation of all others, *was my neglect of the means of Divine grace*, and, most particularly, *my fearful neglect of secret prayer.* Oh, I mourn when I remember how I was wedded to the soul-destructive habit into which I had fallen of drinking to excess! I feared to approach that footstool of mercy where I had often poured out the desires of my soul, and found sweet access to God, and experienced covenant love manifested to my soul.

"One evil led to another: to deceive my best and my Christian friends, and most of all to deceive the wife of my bosom, who is (blessed be God!) a true Christian, I admit was hard work. I had to call forth all my wicked ingenuity and craft to do the work of the devil; and a dreadful drudgery I found it. Oh, it is an evil and a bitter thing to sin against God! I have found it to be so. May the Lord preserve my soul from evil desires, and enable me fully to yield myself unto Him as one that is alive from the dead, and my members as instruments of righteousness unto God! I madly pursued the desires of the flesh. As I just said, one evil gave birth to another, and I was carried down the torrent, and plunged at length into the vortex of iniquity,—indulging in other vices besides intemperance of drinking; but all of them the companions of my easily-besetting and darling sin. My heart aches; and I need not enumerate the many crimes of which I soon became capable. Oh, the holy Lord only can judge of their aggravation and turpitude! But sweet is the truth of the gospel. It now makes my heart tranquil and peaceful from day to day. I find it not only in 1 John ii. 1, 2, but in many other parts of Scripture. It is a precious cordial to my weak and wavering mind. Were it not for this blessed assurance, I think the remembrance of my past awful career against light, and my most desperate and presumptuous sins against the Holy Lord, and the blessed Saviour who died, I hope, even for wretched me,—I say, were it not for this hope, I think I should sink into utter despair; and especially when I think of the consequences of my sins, as they affect my dear and pious wife, and sweet child, and a whole circle of most respectable friends. . . . But I will, in few words, close a history which is most grievous to my mind; and hope you will excuse my unconnected way of writing; but I feel more than I can express.

"I went on until I found my income would not support my extravagance; and at length, to meet difficulties of my own seeking, I added dishonesty to all my other crimes; and used various sums of money to my own purposes that I had collected from my master's customers. Being at length discovered, and being a considerable defaulter, my employer, most reluctantly, was compelled to prosecute. I had been six years in his service. Previous to taking his situation, I held one for a short time in the city, at Messrs. ——, and I am happy to remember that I was preserved from every dishonest act up to the time I have mentioned. *No praise to me.* I thank the Lord, I was, in His mercy, restrained from outward crimes, so that on my trial I had the benefit of a *previous* good character, and was therefore sentenced to only *seven* years. The Recorder of London, who tried me, most humanely told me he would afford me every opportunity in his power to redeem my forfeited character and respectability. I *hope* I shall; but am helpless in myself. But I believe that those holy principles which the gospel of Christ creates in the renewed mind, will, in the use of means, preserve me in His fear, and make me once more an honourable, useful man and Christian. Gracious Lord! keep me humble before Thee, and watchful; and grant me the true spirit of prayer, ' that I may break Thy laws no more; but love Thee and my fellow-men better than before.'

"During my stay in the *Justitia,* I felt the loss of privileges I once enjoyed of a religious nature; but I bless God for those I here enjoy. Previous to taking my trial, and whilst a prisoner in Horsemonger Jail, I met with great kindness from the Rev. Mr. B——, the pious chaplain. I am sorry to say, I was dreadfully hardened up to this time; but his serious and earnest converse with me, together with his daily instructions from the pulpit, by God's blessing, brought me to a better state of mind.

* * * * "Dear Sir, I thank you for all your kindness to me, and I thank the Lord for all the good I have enjoyed through you! May the Lord bless you, is the humble prayer of me, a poor, but I trust, a saved sinner! (Signed) "W. B."

This statement is full of instruction. While it reminds all Christians of the Divine injunctions, "By faith ye stand;"* "Watch and pray;"† "Let him that thinketh he standeth take heed lest he fall,"‡ it loudly warns all my countrymen to beware of sin,— of all violation of the laws of God and of their country; and exposes *the terribleness of crime and its often-attendant punishment—transportation to the penal colonies.*

On a later occasion, W. B. put into my hands the following succinct account of his recovery to the Lord!

"SALVATION IS OF THE LORD."

"The Lord has been pleased in His rich and free mercy to accompany the word of His grace with the power of His Holy Spirit, read and expounded on board this ship, the *Earl Grey.* . . . . . May the Lord bless and keep us all, and help us to grow in grace, and to persevere in the way of holiness and peace! The Lord has made us the monuments of His mercy. Some of us, the vilest and most hardened, have been humbled, and brought to repentance. In some of us His grace has been displayed in a most

---

* 2 Cor. i. 24. † Matt. xxvi. 41. ‡ 1 Cor. x. 12.

wonderful manner. . . . . . . Not unto man, but unto Thy name, O Lord, be all the glory!

"I came on board this ship very hardened and reckless, having no hope, and destitute of the peace and consolation the gospel only can afford; and for some time I continued in this unhappy state of mind.

"I was taken ill with severe rheumatism, and confined to the hospital; and continued unconcerned about my spiritual and eternal interests until one evening, when two men were reported for improper conduct. It was thought proper to deal with these men in the hospital, instead of doing so, agreeably to the usual practice, on the quarter-deck, and I heard them spoken to most solemnly with reference to the evil nature of sin, and its dreadful consequences if persisted in. My mind became very agitated; I was led to think upon my own wickedness and impenitence in the sight of God. I could not sleep or rest. I remembered I had once professed to be the Lord's, but had fallen by my iniquity. I trembled before a holy God; and the remembrance of my wilful and foolish departure from Jesus Christ, and that my sins had again pierced Him, filled me with misery and despair; in which state I continued until the following morning, when it pleased the Lord, I trust, in answer to earnest prayer, to bring to my mind that of which I had been so long destitute, namely, *peace*. I remembered that Jesus died even for the chief of sinners; and He was pleased, by His Holy Spirit, to send to my mind His own consoling words,—'Peace I leave with you; My peace I give unto you: not as the world giveth give I unto you.' Blessed be the

Lord! He helped me to lay hold of His promise, and with deep heart-felt sorrow, I believe, I poured out my soul in the feelings and language of sincere repentance; and was, by His grace, brought to the Cross, and enabled to put my trust in Him who died thereon: and He gave me that peace, which, blessed be His name, I now enjoy, arising from faith in His justifying righteousness, and precious, cleansing blood. I can now rejoice in the Lord, and my heart is desirous still more to love Him who first loved me, and hath drawn me by His cords of love to receive Him as the Father's unspeakable gift. To Him, I look, and on Him depend, for salvation from the power and indwelling of sin. I have no other hope or Saviour but Jesus, neither do I desire to have. If I know myself, my anxious inquiry is, *Lord, what wilt Thou have me to do?* Oh, that He would make use of me as an instrument of good to my dear fellow-sinners, and help me to glorify my heavenly Father by bringing forth much fruit! May I be kept by his power, through faith, unto salvation! My own wisdom, strength, and righteousness, I feel, by daily experience, will not avail; for I have nothing to trust in but the Lord Jesus, who of God is made unto me wisdom, righteousness, sanctification, and redemption. I can trust in the Lord *generally*, though fear and unbelief sometimes creep in, and rob me of my peace. But, thanks to the Lord for his Divine mercy to me, a vile sinner!

"I am not troubled for the future, even in my present unhappy situation as a prisoner. The Lord, I believe, will support and comfort me, for he has said so: 'Casting all our care upon Him, for He careth for you,' is a stay to my mind. Oh, may I be watchful and prayerful, and enabled to cleave unto him; and may I meet dear Dr. B—— in heaven, to enjoy and praise our glorious Lord in one perpetual rest for ever, through sovereign grace! Amen, and Amen."

It will be remembered how my purpose, that this man should not sail in the *Earl Grey*, was overruled. In the course of the voyage he stated to me, that, before he had seen me, or knew any thing of the system of instruction and discipline that would be in operation in that transport, his desire to embark in her was so strong and peculiar that he could not express it in language. Although by the tenderest ties his heart was knit to home, he could not repress his extraordinary, and at the time unaccountable, wish to embark in the *Earl Grey*, for conveyance to the land in which he was justly doomed to pass seven years of most dishonourable and revolting bondage.

His gratitude for the goodness and mercy of the Lord towards him during the voyage was most deep, ardent, and devout; and I had scarcely less cause of thankfulness to the Father of mercies for his assistance in the spiritual instruction and improvement of the people.

It will be remembered that we sailed from Plymouth Sound on the 5th October. It was on December 8th that the *eleven* men made a public profession of their faith in Christ, and of their purpose, in His strength, to cultivate holiness in heart and life. Up to this period, W— B— was employed as a schoolmaster, and

I believe that he had not neglected opportunities of drawing the attention of his fellow prisoners to the gospel, although he had not yet manifested that remarkable zeal by which he was afterwards distinguished. This may have been caused by the delicate state of his health, and by his sense of peculiar guilt as a backslider from that God and Saviour whose love he had early tasted.

In addition to our morning and evening reading and exposition of sacred Scripture, with accompanying devotional exercises, I had commenced a series of popular lectures on Geography, &c., in order to lead the people to contemplate the perfections of God in the material creation, in connexion with the study of His Divine attributes in the pages of inspiration. I had also begun an explanatory and practical exposition of the Epistle to the Romans. Our examination of the people one by one, in regular order, took place as often as other urgent duties admitted; and in no instance did we neglect to make special inquiry into their acquaintance with the scriptural way of salvation.

For some time my mind had been greatly oppressed by the consideration that our voyage was rapidly advancing towards its termination, and that, although their general deportment was so serious and pleasing, such scanty evidence of a *decided* character had as yet been afforded of a work of Divine grace in the hearts of the prisoners. From the period of my appointment my mind had been more or less deeply impressed by the great truth, that the conversion of the soul to God by the faith of Christ is exclusively the work of the Holy Spirit, and in our daily intercourse and prayers, I do not think that this Divine truth had ever been lost sight of. But the necessity of *special*, earnest, and believing prayer for the abundant effusion of the Spirit of all grace, was, as the voyage advanced, more deeply felt; and as individual prisoners turned to the Lord, they were implored to make the promised gift of the Holy Spirit the special subject of their supplications at the throne of grace. Thus prayer, both secret and social, with a particular reference to this subject, became more prevalent and fervent.

What an event is the conversion of a soul unto God; for the accomplishment of which the beloved Son of God came into the world and died, and for which the Holy Ghost was promised and sent. What is the planting of an earthly monarchy, when compared with the deliverance of an immortal soul from sin and death—excepting, indeed, as such a monarchy may be made subservient to the extension of the Redeemer's kingdom? What is the grand end supposed to be answered in the Divine dispensations by this voyage? Not the mere conveyance of 264 men, for their crimes, to a remote corner of the world. The great design, whatever subordinate ends may be secured, is unquestionably the advancement of the reign and glory of Christ, in the conversion of souls through the power of His gospel.

The people were more and more closely and earnestly dealt with in reference to their individual and personal safety in Christ Jesus. They were urged to bring their belief, their hearts, their practice, to the test of inspired Scripture; to be faithful to each other; to recollect that each is his "brother's keeper;* that they are responsible to God for their influence upon one another; that each is bound to give himself to Christ without delay; and, without delay, labour to win to Christ all to whom he has lawful access.

The glory of God in the salvation of the soul, and its advancement in Divine knowledge and holiness, obviously became the all-absorbing concern of a great body of the people. All things else took their proper place in our consideration, and in the employment of our time. My private conversations with the impressed and inquiring, became more frequent, and passing incidents were earnestly turned to the highest account.

Practical, solemn addresses on seasonable and appropriate subjects from Scripture were delivered as frequently as strength and other engagements permitted, and the blessing of the Lord, which alone maketh rich, and with which he addeth no sorrow,† was not withheld from us. Blessed and praised for ever be His holy name!

On Dec. 14th, the people seemed impressed by an address founded on Ezek. xxxiv., particularly verses 11—16. On the day following, the subject of solemn address was *Death;* suggested by the death of John Williams, referred to, Chap. iii.; and on the 16th, 1st Corinth. xv. was expounded at morning and evening

---

* Gen. iv. 9; Lev. xix. 17.   † Prov. x. 22.

worship. On this day the number of men who appeared truly to have embraced Christ as all their salvation and all their desire, and to have taken up His cross to follow Him, had increased to *twenty-four*.

On Saturday, the 17th, between two and three o'clock in the afternoon, *thirty-five* of the people assembled in the ward, all of whom had either received Christ in truth or expressed a desire to be found among His true and faithful followers. They were all briefly addressed in reference to the profession they had made, considered in its relation to *God* and to *man*, especially to their fellow-prisoners. Yesterday and to-day, one of the people, at my request, engaged in prayer, and with peculiar propriety and great acceptance.

Dec. 18th was the Lord's day; and a most solemn and memorable day it was to us on board the *Earl Grey*. The state of the weather rendered it necessary that we should assemble for church below in the prison. Nearly the whole of the people had met of their own accord in the morning, immediately after breakfast, to read the Scriptures, and engage in social prayer for the Lord's gracious presence, and the outpouring of His Spirit upon us when assembled at church. As I entered the prison for church, I found one of the petty officers just concluding the third chapter of Malachi. They had begun their worship with singing the Morning Hymn. My mind was most agreeably impressed by this voluntary demonstration of the people's desire to worship God, to edify one another, and to seek the salvation of souls on board. The scene, as I entered the door, was truly impressive. A deep seriousness pervaded the assembly. We *prayed* the Litany; and I hope the Lord was with us, and was truly worshipped.

In the afternoon service, the captain of the second division recited, with the most perfect accuracy, the whole of the Sermon on the Mount. Being called to attend to other duties, the meeting was concluded by W. B—r reading to the people a section of my address to the Irish women transported to Sydney, under my care, in the year 1840. In the evening, after some remarks on 1 John iii., which had been recited in the afternoon, the people's attention was drawn to certain expressions in their communications to me, which clearly implied great *legality* of sentiment and feeling, in reference to their salvation—such as, "I have resolved to do my utmost;" "I mean to commence a new course;" "I have resolved" to do this, and to do that, and the like, which expressions imply a want of perception of the *presentness, freeness,* and *perfection* of the salvation of the Son of God, as set forth in the Scriptures, for example in Romans x. and John iii.— a blindness to the truth, that Jesus the Saviour is the *free* and unspeakable *gift* of the Father to guilty, lost, and helpless sinners. The subject was illustrated by reference to a debtor offered a full and free discharge from his debt. The discharge is held out to him; it is close to him; he is simply to accept of it as a gift; it is offered to him *now*, it is pressed upon his acceptance, and he is required *without a moment's delay* to accept of it, for the purposes for which it is given. A man is perishing of hunger: bread, without money and without price, is set before him; he is implored to receive it, to eat and live: does he say, Well, I am determined, when I get on shore, or to the colony, or am placed in other circumstances, I will most strenuously labour to obtain this bread, that I perish not? Why, it is presented to him *now!* He needs it *now!* It is a *gift!* It cannot be bought. It is the free gift of his Sovereign. And so is the salvation of the gospel. The serpent-bitten Jew in the wilderness looks, simply looks, in faith, to the serpent lifted up on the pole, and in looking is healed, and lives! The Philippian jailer, overwhelmed with guilt and fear, cries, "What must I do to be saved?" He is told to believe on the Lord Jesus Christ; he believes, and is saved, and immediately obtains peace and joy.

Divine worship concluded on this most interesting day with singing the hymn,—

> Not all the blood of beasts
>   On Jewish altars slain,
> Could give the guilty conscience peace,
>   Or wash away the stain.
>
> But Christ the heavenly Lamb!
>   Takes all our sins away,
> A sacrifice of nobler name,
>   And richer blood than they.

From my Journal, I make the following extract:

"The number of prisoners on board the *Earl Grey* who have either believed on the Lord Jesus Christ, or profess to be earnestly seeking an interest in His great salvation, amounts, this day, to *forty-seven:* all of whom regularly meet together at stated times for the reading of the Scriptures, social prayer, and praise.

"All glory be ascribed to the Father, and the Son, and the Holy Ghost, both now and for evermore. Amen."

On the day following, I received information of another man being under deep concern about his best interests, but my numerous and urgent duties not permitting me to converse with him myself, I could only appoint W— B— to do so in the mean time: and it was a great relief to my mind that the Lord had been graciously pleased to provide and qualify a man whom I could employ in such sacred work, and in whose spiritual discernment, judgment, and integrity, I could place such entire confidence. The peculiarities of individual cases afforded subject of *general* instruction, calculated, under the Divine blessing, to benefit all the people, as well as the persons more immediately in view. But whatever might be those peculiarities, we never ceased to keep before the minds of all, the scriptural answer to that all-engrossing question, "*How can God be just in justifying the ungodly who believe in Jesus?*" Their responsibility for the exercise of their will and affections is urged upon them; and the iniquity, folly, and danger of delaying, for an instant, their grateful and joyous reception of Christ for all the ends for which He is given, is so unceasingly pressed upon them, that they cannot escape from the thought that either they have *received* the Son of God, or are *rejecting* Him every hour; that they are voluntarily *yielding* to the Holy Spirit's persuasive dealings with them, or are *resisting* Him, and most wickedly putting Him away from them.

This chapter I shall conclude with brief notices of two men who appeared to have turned to God, by the faith of His Son, Jesus Christ:

F. M., twenty-seven years of age, and brought up in the habits of a farm-labourer, was one of those men who received their entire education on board the *Earl Grey*. On Oct. 11th, he was taken ill, was for some time confined to the hospital, and lay close to John Williams; whose death has been noticed. Of himself he says,—

" All my life I have been living in sin and crime, a hardened man. But I have reason to be thankful that I came here. The Lord afflicted me and brought me very low: but, thanks be to His name! He has raised me up again. I thought nothing about my soul until I was getting well; and when serious things troubled me I put them out of my mind as soon as I could. I had often talked to John Williams, who lay near me in the hospital; but nothing particular occurred until the day on which he was *buried in the sea*. I was then very much affected; and I thought, had it been *me* instead of Williams, I must have been lost for ever! These thoughts led me to pray, and, I hope, sincerely. My feelings I cannot describe; I never felt the like before. But I remembered what had been often told us on board, and I was reading in my testament every day, '*that Jesus died to save sinners, even the chief.*' But I did not know how to pray; the distress increased, until I felt forced to cry to Him—O Lord, save me, and wash me in Thy blood! I seemed instantly a new man—I *could believe on Him!* I feel still very weak, and disposed often to do what is evil. Blessed Lord! keep me near to Thee, and make me a true and living servant of Thine."

This poor man had been taught to read his Bible on board; and although his mind had not greatly expanded, his power of thinking, and of thinking profitably, had greatly increased; his whole appearance had most obviously improved, and his spirit, manners, and conduct, corresponded with his profession of the Christian faith.

Towards the end of the voyage, when suffering severely from the effects of fatigue and care, I received the following letter from a young man, about twenty-two years of age, who had received some education, and whose appearance and manners were rather prepossessing, but who, though so young, had, by his great folly, and criminal waywardness, brought a heavy load of guilt upon his conscience, and subjected his relations to much shame and suffering. The letter is dated Dec. 23, 1842:

. . . . . "My father died when I was about two years old. My dear mother, who still lives, and who fears the Lord, endeavoured to bring me up in His fear. I was sent to Mr. J.'s sabbath-school; and I shall not forget the instructions I there received in my youthful days, while I have the power of memory. My dear mother used to direct my mind to the Scriptures, and especially to the book of Proverbs. She was acquainted with the family of Mr. L—, and used to send me to their house when I had got off any thing by heart from the Bible, when Mr. S. L. used to hear me and give me very good advice; which if I had but taken, how happy I might have been!

"At twelve years of age I was apprenticed. My master was far from being a religious man, and cared not how I spent my sabbaths,—whether I went to a place of worship or not. I forgot all the good advice of kind friends, and used to break the sabbath by going on the water, and pursuing many bad ways. At nineteen years of age, I left him, and was pushed into the wicked world, without any care for my soul. At this time I was working for a Mr. J. L—. Mrs. L. senior noticed me, and wished me to go and see her, which I did. She gave me some very good counsel, which, though I sadly neglected, I can never forget, and have often reflected upon it since I came on board this ship, and am grieved at my heart I have acted so contrary to it. That kind and very pious lady recommended me to go to Mr. B.'s chapel; which I did for some time. But my heart aches when I think how I forsook the house of God, where I had found profit,—closed my eyes to the light, and my ears to the instruction of the Holy Scriptures, and of Divine ordinances; and, although I was getting a very honourable living at my trade, working for a good master, and might have done as well as any young man in every respect, yet I, like a madman, threw away every privilege and advantage, and brought misery upon myself, and on my best friends I brought sorrow; and most of all *upon my mother!*

"I joined some wicked companions; was soon led into all manner of wicked ways; became dishonest;

got into prison; came out again *no better;* and was very soon taken up again for another robbery; was tried, and sentenced to seven years' transportation: and here I am grieved, and now, I hope, humbled before God.

"Up to the night of Nov. 2d, when that dreadful storm was sent by the Almighty, I continued, notwithstanding all I suffered, quite hardened, and as thoughtless as ever. But on that night I was very frightened, and expected the thunder and lightning were sent to destroy all of us wicked creatures, and I expected to die; but I knew I was not fit to die, and should go to hell with all my sins on my head unpardoned. The terror of mind I felt, I cannot tell. All the day following my past sins stared me in the face; and I felt I needed some one to save me from the dreadful doom which I richly deserved.

"It was then I thought of Jesus Christ, of whom I had heard, but had almost entirely forgotten: and to the Lord Jesus Christ I was directed to lift up my soul, by my messmate, who lay by my side, and exhorted me to search the Bible, that I might there read of His great love to the worst of sinners. I read the 1st, 3rd, and 15th chapters of John's Gospel; and I thank and praise the Lord, I have found, to my soul's comfort and peace, Him of whom Moses in the Law and the Prophets did write, Jesus Christ, to whom I was enabled to come, just the vile wretch I felt myself to be; and He did not turn me away, but enabled me to receive and embrace Him by the faith He was pleased to give me. And now I love Him, I hope, and put my whole trust in Him for my salvation!

"I feel very weak and very ignorant; but I bless God I feel I get fresh strength as I am enabled daily to come to the Lord, with humility, I hope. I sincerely thank Him for the great good I received through your instrumentality. I delight to hear you explain the Scriptures to us, and find great profit and comfort; and I trust through grace to persevere in this good way. And I believe that to all eternity I shall have cause to praise God that I was placed under your care on board the *Earl Grey*.

"Please let me ask you to pray for me, that I may be kept holy, humble, and useful to my fellow-men. Oh, may I be a useful and a respectable man where I am going, and wherever I may spend my days!

"May the Lord support you under all your sorrows, and give you peace, and make you a great blessing to us all, is the prayer of your grateful, and humble, and obedient servant, "J. S."

Of *one thousand and sixty-five* prisoners who have in five different voyages, been conveyed under my superintendence to the Penal Colonies of Australia, *fourteen* only had been educated at a sabbath-school; of which J. S— was one.

His history reminds us of the duty and responsibility of masters in reference to their apprentices and shopmen. How immense the amount of good which the truly pious, prudent, and zealous master may be the means, through believing prayer and the supply of the

Holy Spirit, of effecting for those whom God has placed under his authority and moral influence! This is a subject which all masters are called to consider; to consider in the light of Scripture,—in the light of the judgment day,—in the light of a guilty world on fire, and melting with fervent heat,—in the light of hell,—in the light of heaven—the light of an endless eternity!

We see what great benefit one messmate,—one fellow-apprentice, or fellow servant,—one shipmate, or comrade,—one schoolfellow,—one acquaintance, or friend,—one fellow-prisoner, may, under the blessing of God, confer upon another. And we are solemnly reminded that God requires all men, in their respective stations in life, to be habitually on the watch for opportunities of winning souls to Christ.

The following short paper, chiefly relating to the change in this young man's views and character, was put into my hands by one of his fellow-prisoners, and although it repeats some of the statements contained in his letter, it appears to deserve a place in this narrative:

J. S— says, "I have spent the whole of my life in the service of the wicked one, following after the pleasure of this world, and living without so much as a thought of my condition as a sinner in the sight of God. In this state I continued until I came on board this ship. I had no concern about my soul, or the course of sin and crime I had so eagerly pursued.

"On the night of November the 2nd, during our voyage, we were visited by a dreadful thunder-storm.

The lightning descended upon the ship, which appeared to be on fire; and had not the Almighty dispersed the electric fluid, we must have perished. As it was, the visitation was very awful. I was so alarmed that I durst not stir, and every moment I expected *death!* In this state I continued for some time, fearing to die. A messmate who lay by me begged of me to pray, and to flee to the only refuge of sinners, Jesus Christ! I had never prayed in *reality* in my life. But now I was, I hope, for the first time, taught of God to pray from the heart, and to cry out, 'God be merciful to me a sinner!' I was very unhappy for some days; but still I prayed that I might know Jesus Christ, and put my trust in Him. One evening, when at prayer, I felt something like a load removed from my heart, and I was enabled to come unto the Saviour, who promised that He would in nowise cast out any that come unto Him. I was deeply wounded on account of my past wickedness; but I was glad in Him who died to save sinners. I had an humble hope that He died for me, *even for me!*

"I desire still to cleave unto the Lord, and to love and serve Him who has done so much for me. I thank God my soul is often refreshed by the worship of the Lord on board. The Bible I once disregarded I now love. I am truly thankful I ever came on board this ship. God's providence directed me here. I trust never to forget the kind instructions I daily receive on board the *Earl Grey:* I thank the Lord for the officer placed over us. May I, through grace, be enabled to go on in the strength of Jesus Christ, as one of His true and devoted followers!"

This young man, from the day his heart was opened to receive the Gospel, up to the day he landed in the colony, was enabled to maintain a most consistent and irreproachable character.

CHAPTER V.

More earnest prayer for the promised gift of the Holy Spirit—Hospital patients, J. H., W. C., T. G., and John Walker—Written statements from James B., Robert T., R. R—k.

NOTWITHSTANDING that we had now great cause of gratitude and praise to the God of all grace for His infinite mercy vouchsafed to so many of the prisoners, through the knowledge of His Son Jesus Christ, and were daily sent to His footstool to adore Him for the manifestations of His love and pardoning mercy to one prisoner after another, and although nearly the whole of the people seemed more or less under Divine influence, and concerned for their best interests, yet the consideration that so many still afforded no decided evidence of being "brought to themselves," and of turning heart and feet towards their Father's house, tended to fill the mind with deep anxiety, to excite to more earnest, wrestling prayer for the farther outpouring of the Holy Spirit, and to call forth still greater efforts to instruct them in the Holy Scriptures, and to urge upon their consciences their responsibility and spiritual danger.

On Tuesday, Dec. 28, at two o'clock in the afternoon, the people were assembled below for *extra* examination on their possession of *saving knowledge.* Before our catechetical exercises commenced, we were incidentally led to address the whole of the prisoners, on Christianity viewed under *the aspect it wears to convicts,* and to impress upon them not only that all they have to comfort and sustain them in their sufferings, during the remainder of their life, and in the hour of death, is to be found in the Divine system of Christianity; but that it tends to make all who are brought under its sanctifying power, kind and faithful friends to them. Men of the world *may* treat them harshly, and at this they must not be surprised, but submit without even "answering again;" but real Christians will ever, when acting in character, deal with them truly and tenderly, and will seek to promote their truest happiness. They were solemnly cautioned against professing Christianity hypocritically, or merely for the sake of any worldly advantage. We learn, indeed, from the Scriptures, the immense advantages which even in this life, are infallibly secured to all who, in very deed, are vitally united by faith to Jesus Christ; because "godliness is profitable unto *all* things, having the promise of the life that now is," as well as "of that which is to come."* But it is the Lord *Himself* we are urged to choose as our present and eternal inheritance; while we are faithfully reminded, that if any man will live godly in Christ Jesus, he shall suffer persecution; and that it is through much tribulation that Christians are to enter the kingdom of God.

* 1 Tim. iv. 8.

Our catechetical examinations became more and more interesting; tending greatly to increase my acquaintance with the spiritual wants, as well as the attainments, of the people; and enabling them to make a more just estimate of themselves. These examinations seemed not only deeply to excite the interest of the people, but to afford them much more distinct and available knowledge than mere lectures and addresses.

My hospital, at this time, presented a most interesting, and really affecting appearance. Each of its six sleeping-berths was occupied by a patient from the prisoners. In one berth lay a most unhappy young man, named J— H—, who was a source of great vexation and perplexity to me during the last two thirds of the voyage. He was excessively ignorant; of a most wayward disposition; indolent in the extreme; irregular in his habits; and ever ready to break through established regulations. At length, his depravity having assumed a most unhappy and threatening aspect, he became, in my view, a proper subject for hospital care and watchfulness.

I often reasoned kindly and solemnly with this man, with the hope of bringing him to a right state of mind; and the most intelligent of the prisoners, who had some influence over him, often exerted themselves to bring him to think and act aright; but all in vain. To speak to him seemed speaking to the air. His mind was fortified against all the arguments of reason, and all the declarations, threatenings, and promises of Divine revelation;—and his conscience seemed lulled into the sleep of death! He had been brought up amongst a people who had filled his mind with prejudices against the word of God. For the one and only object of Divine worship and adoration, the great Jehovah, he had been taught to substitute myriads of created beings, male and female, who themselves were called into existence to give glory to God, not to rob Him of His due; and who have no power to deliver, even if they could hear his idolatrous cry. For the absolution of his sins, he had been directed to look also to sinful creatures, who can neither absolve themselves nor the unhappy beings whom they delude; and who, by their daring presumption, only augment the fearful amount of their guilt, while they consign to perdition the souls whom they deceive. The thought of a simple, direct, and believing application to the Lord Jesus Christ, the Divine and only High Priest of the one Church of the living God, for pardon, peace, and acceptance with God, was one wholly alien to his misled and benighted mind. The kingdom of God, which consisteth not in meat and drink, but in righteousness, peace, and joy in the Holy Ghost, he seemed to have been *religiously* instructed *devoutly* to oppose! In a word, he was in the trammels of a system which is diametrically opposed to the revealed will of the Lord Jesus Christ, the Great Head of the Church; a system which substitutes the doctrines, ordinances, and commandments of men for those of God; and which tends ignominiously to prostrate the human mind, to destroy the bonds of social confidence, and to engender all that is oppressive, cruel, and revolting; a system which is inimical to the best interests of society, to the prosperity of any country, the security of any Government, and the stability of any earthly empire; which originated in darkness, tends to darkness, loves darkness, and hates that "True Light" before which it cannot stand; a system from the entanglements of which it is the purest benevolence to afford deliverance.

Let the people of God, in fervent prayer and devout adherence to inspired truth, watch against the wiles of Satan, the father of lies, as he is now stealthily manifesting himself among us as an angel of light, spreading his net with consummate art, to entrap the unstable of every class, particularly those persons whose pride and vanity, whose feelings and imaginations, render them peculiarly liable to be taken in his toils, and as peculiarly fit to become his instruments in the fearful work of entangling souls, and ensuring their everlasting perdition.

Here is the consolation of the saints: "When the enemy shall come in like a flood, the Spirit of the Lord shall lift up a standard against him."* And the "man of sin," that "wicked one," the whole "mystery of iniquity," "shall the Lord consume with the Spirit of His mouth, and shall destroy with the brightness of His coming."†

How different the character, condition, and hopes of the remaining five men, who, at this time, occupied the other berths in my hospital, to those of poor J. H—; whom we could only pity and pray for, while we used every means to impart good both to his body and his soul.

* Isa. lix. 19. † 2 Thess. ii. 3, 7, 8—17.

One berth was occupied by *George Day*, to whom we have already made the most gratifying reference. He always appeared humble, contented, and resigned; grateful to God for the abundance of His mercies; frequently engaged in praying, reading, or listening to his Bible; and ever happy in the faith of Jesus Christ his Lord.

In a second berth lay W. B—tt, who was recovering from a dangerous attack of inflammation: his mind had been gradually enlightened by Divine truth; he always seemed remarkably contented, and experienced much spiritual joy and peace.

A third bed was occupied by a lad named W— C—, about nineteen years of age; who had lain for a considerable time apparently at the gates of death, and whose recovery was very remarkable. Although he was one of those who did not know their letters when they embarked; and though he was cut off from his school and his book by sickness, for a considerable portion of the voyage; he was able, long before it terminated, to read the New Testament with fluency. The zeal of this youth was quite extraordinary. The book seemed never out of his hand. I have often been amused and gratified, on entering the hospital at night: W. C. was sure to wake up at the light of my lantern, and quietly slipping his New Testament from under his pillow, he did not close it till the light was withdrawn.

His disposition was meek and amiable. He seemed to have been divinely taught the deceitfulness of his own heart, and to have been drawn by the cords of love to the feet of Jesus, there to confess his iniquities, and obtain the forgiveness and peace which His atoning blood alone can give. His conduct was marked by child-like simplicity, and uniform consistency, while he remained under my authority and observation.

A fourth berth was occupied by T— G—, a man who had been of considerable use to me as a teacher, and who, from his sedate appearance, his manly carriage, good sense, and habitually excellent behaviour, had obtained considerable influence amongst his fellow-prisoners. In a short note which he wrote to me some time before the debarkation took place, he says:

"I was born at Ch—n, a small village in Warwickshire; of honest, kind, and godly parents, who did all in their power to bring me up to love and to fear the Lord, and gave me a very good education, in teaching me to read the Bible with ease and comfort to myself, and to the approbation of those who heard me; a circumstance which, in the early part of my life, seemed to yield them great comfort. But it pleased the Lord to deprive me, by death, of both my parents when I was yet young; and thus was I left without an earthly friend! But the Lord was a friend to me, and I was very well respected by all the good people in the village. On the Lord's day I always attended Divine worship, and was induced to join the choir, and play the clarionet.* I continued to be respected by the

---

* I would remind Christians of the impropriety of employing unconverted men or women, to assist in conducting the music with which the church essays to worship God: a practice most unscriptural and unapostolic, converting immortal and accountable beings, (often the *dissi-*

good and pious people in the parish for several years; when I thought proper to enter into the marriage state. But my respectability did not continue, for during the last six or seven years I have led a very wicked course of life, which began by my joining a band of musicians; a step which brought great disgrace upon my character; and I became so fond of music, that I was always at some club-feast or election; some wake or fair; or was at some public-house, playing at a ball or dance; by which conduct I greatly degraded myself. Instead of being at my work as I used to be, I was never found there when I was wanted, and by so acting I lost all my business; and this proved fatal to me; for I soon found that I could not get work to do, and speedily I had no food in my house to support life; and ere long, by this wicked course, I was led to steal, and soon found myself in the county jail: to which, for my first offence, I was sentenced for six months.

"When I obtained my liberty, my circumstances were not improved, for the people saw no reformation in me. I could scarcely find any work to do, and was soon led again to break the laws of my country; and for this I received sentence of transportation for seven years;—a sentence which took some effect upon my mind: but when I came to the hulk and saw so much wickedness, my heart became more hardened;

pated and *licentious*,) into mere musical instruments to be used in Divine worship. Bring them to Jesus, let His spiritual reign be set up in their souls, and then, with the whole body of true worshippers, they will sing the song of salvation and praise, with a cheerful voice, and a sanctified heart. 1 Cor. xiv. 15.

for I thought if other people live in sin, I may live so too. But when I came on board the *Earl Grey*, under your kind instruction, and heard the gospel sounded in my ears, I began to see and feel myself a sinner, and that I needed a Saviour to pardon my sins, and to give peace and comfort to my guilty soul: and I have great reason to thank God that I was placed under your care; for it was by your prayers and reading the Holy Scriptures, that I was brought to a knowledge of that Saviour who is able to make us wise unto salvation."

This brief history is full of instruction, and affords much seasonable warning and caution:

1. It may warn Christian parents not to be *satisfied* with any improvement in their children that falls short of *conversion to God:* nothing else can keep them from falling into sin.

2. It is calculated to impress the minds of magistrates with the awful responsibility which attaches to their office; and calls upon them seriously to consider the probable effects of imprisonment upon the character and future prospects of those who are brought before them, those especially who are accused of some petty offence—their first, or second, it may be; committed, too, perhaps, (however *unjustifiably*) through the pressure of starvation. The question should be, not merely what does the law require; but what will it admit of,* as calculated to recover the offender, and

---

* If the law of the land should not in every instance admit of the offender being wisely dealt with, our legislators are called to lay the matter to heart.

promote the best interests of society? If the man's history be duly inquired into and considered—if he be judiciously and kindly reprimanded and advised; a faithful subject may be preserved to the Queen, and a useful member to the community.

If, on the other hand, the magistrate send the transgressor to *prison*, an *immortal being* may be *ruined for ever!* The prison may be to him the charnel-house of souls! The bolting of the prison door may be, in the relation of moral cause and effect, the barring upon him for ever of the iron gates of hell! He is stripped of nearly all he most values as an Englishman. He feels he has lost the respect of his friends and neighbours, and of mankind, and therefore loses all respect for himself. When freed from imprisonment, he is not freed from infamy, scorn, and self-contempt. The means of providing for his wife and family are gone; and being a stranger to Christianity, he is criminally induced again to steal; and the result is, that awfully destructive punishment of transportation—a punishment which tends, in ordinary circumstances, and especially if the transgressor be a woman, to the eternal loss of the soul.

3. This case further shows us the importance of providing prisoners with suitable employment, when restored to freedom, until they can obtain work for themselves.

Lastly: Let all men beware of forsaking or neglecting the duties of their proper calling: of associating with companions, or indulging in habits, which lead to penury, dishonesty, and crime; which involve infamy and suffering, and the untold terribleness of transportation, if not even death; and which habits tend to the eternal destruction of the soul!

The carriage of T. G. was *most satisfactory*, as far as my observation extended; and it was pleasant to join with him in devotional exercises, for, as far as man could see, he possessed both the gift and the grace of social prayer.

John Walker, a man who always appeared deeply affected and depressed by the disgrace he had brought upon himself, was the remaining prisoner of the six who occupied the hospital at the time to which I refer. He had served for many years in the army, and belonged to a regiment of cavalry, in which he rose to the rank of troop-sergeant. He was in the battle of Waterloo, served for some time in India, and was engaged in the last Burmese war. Although he was only fifty-six years of age, he had a much older appearance; and his constitution had evidently suffered much from hard service and tropical climates. His tall figure (about six feet three inches high) and his military gait tended to arrest attention, and he became a special object of observation, by invariably taking up his position at church close to the after-side of the mainmast, against which he leaned, preferring to stand during the whole time of Divine worship; and being very deaf, he kept his hand behind his ear to facilitate the collection of sound. Among the prisoners on the quarter-deck he was, therefore, a prominent figure; and to all that was read or spoken he seemed to listen with an unrelaxed and devouring attention.

He occasionally suffered from derangement of the digestive system during the voyage, and on Dec. 1st was entered on the sick list and received into the hospital. It was then he came more immediately under my close and daily observation; and no language of mine can describe the interesting state of his mind, or the satisfaction and delight with which I watched his progress in Divine knowledge and grace. He knew not the way of salvation when he embarked in the *Earl Grey*, and possessed no sound and salutary knowledge of himself. He stated to me that pride and ambition had been the ruling passions of his life. His heart had been set on nothing but rising in the army, and securing approbation and applause as a soldier. I had such respect for his feelings, that I could never so remind him of his degradation as a convict, as to inquire into the circumstances which led to it. The immediate cause of his transportation was, if I mistake not, some act of petty larceny. No conduct could be more circumspect and manly than his uniformly was, on board the transport. And now that his heavenly Father had, in a double stroke, laid upon him His chastening hand, and was leading him by His word and Spirit to see his true character as a guilty, depraved, and helpless sinner, and to perceive the beauty and excellency of Christ, the suitableness, freeness, and *nearness* of His great salvation,—disposing him to look up from the dust into which he had been prostrated, and by faith to behold His beloved Son suffering and dying upon the accursed tree as a sacrifice for the sins of men,—I do not think I ever witnessed such a beautiful mixture of humility and self-abasement, with believing confidence, and gratitude, and peace, and entire resignation to the Divine will, as appeared in this worn and outcast soldier. It was an unspeakable pleasure to all around him to show him kindness and attention, and his deep and grateful sense of every kind service was at once gratifying to his attendants and illustrative of his Christian character. Although it was very difficult to converse with him, on account of his deafness, it was always most delightful to do so. No heart could remain unmoved under the contemplation of this old and *once* proud warrior, now exhibiting the spirit of a little child; looking to Jesus, as at once his fortress and refuge, and the almighty Captain of his salvation,—the large tears involuntarily running down his weather-beaten cheeks, while he spoke of his blessed Saviour's love and sympathy, and magnified the riches of His grace. He marvelled at the movement of the wheels of holy Providence, placing him in the *Earl Grey*, to hear that blessed Gospel which the Spirit of all grace had made effectual to the saving of his soul, although he had so long despised and neglected it. Of this exhausted and emaciated sufferer it could be truly affirmed, that "*the joy of the Lord was his strength.*"

On arrival at Hobart, he was sent to the Colonial Hospital, where, under the tender and watchful care of the Christian medical officer formerly alluded to, he died, in the continued enjoyment of that peace which the atoning blood of Christ can alone impart.

From this time my hospital was never without two

or three men, or more, who, taking the places of those now alluded to, appeared to derive their chief happiness from the enjoyment of God, in His word, and in prayer and other spiritual exercises. Never, in any ship, did I enter daily my hospital with such peculiar and happy feelings; I ever felt I was ministering to members of the household of faith, plucked by the Eternal Spirit as brands out of the fire; and constituted monuments of mercy, that all who hear of such manifestations of Divine grace might be rescued from the sin and danger of despair, and throw themselves on the mercy of God in Christ, the Divine Head of the better covenant.*

A notice of each of the prisoners on board the *Earl Grey*, who were apparently brought back unto God by the faith of His Gospel, could not fail to interest all who feel the value of the soul and a concern for the glory of Christ: but my unceasing and anxious labours did not afford me time to make memoranda of all the cases of reformation which presented themselves; and even from those I possess, the limits of this narrative do not allow me to select many more.

To one young man, named James B—, I must allude, whose entire life, from his boyhood till he came on board the *Earl Grey*, seems to have been filled up with vice and crime, and affords a most melancholy exemplification of that saying of the wise and inspired monarch, "One sinner destroyeth much good,"† and therefore inflicts much evil. Vast, then,

---

* 2 Sam. xxiii. 5; Psa. lxxxix.   † Eccles. ix. 18.

must be the benefits, which the conversion to God of even one sinner, confers upon his country and upon the moral world.

After he came under spiritual instruction in the transport, his evil principles and habits seemed for some time to have disputed every inch of ground, both with reason and conscience; and for several weeks he continued to vacillate under convictions of right and wrong, between *the bondage of sin and Satan,* and *the holy liberty of the Son of God;* but after reciting, one Sabbath afternoon, the fifty-third of Isaiah, he began to cry to the Lord more earnestly than before, and continued daily thus to pray, until he obtained some measure of help and deliverance. In this way he went on until the fearful night of the 2nd of November, when God's voice in the fierce thunderbolt met His voice in His inspired word, and made the guilty and wretched transgressor deeply to feel that nothing could avail him but "*Salvation through faith in Jesus Christ.*"

In a written communication to me, this young man gives the following account of himself:

"I am a native of S—, near Huddersfield, and was born in 1819. I am a weaver by trade. My mother was a very pious woman, and took delight in sending me to the Sunday-school, and bringing me up in the knowledge and love of God. On the contrary, my father was a very great drunkard and a very wicked man, and more is the pity. My mother died in 1832. Up to that time, I was brought up under the rod; after this, my father got worse and worse. Myself and a younger brother were the main support of the family. My father used to spend part of our earnings, and caused us to go short of food; it used to grieve me, and I got so hardened that I thought I would not work any more, and I used to go gambling, and began to steal apples, and from that to fowls. After that, I thought it was time to give up such wicked ways, and that I would go to my married brother, and see if he would let me live with him. He received me kindly, and got me a job of weaving; but after a considerable time my father fetched me home again. I had not been there long, before I fell into my old thievish tricks, and got more wicked than ever; so I went to one of my acquaintances, and we agreed to rob a public-house. We got away without suspicion: but after that, I never went to bed without conscience telling me I had done wrong; every footstep I heard, for months, I thought was the constables after me. At this time I was about sixteen years of age. Well, I thought if I could only once more make myself safe, I would give up such ways; so I went to my brother's, worked very hard, and earned a great deal of money: but I took to going to public-houses and spending my money at cards, till trade failed, then I came to be in want of what I had spent at cards. I then got acquainted with bad company, and started off on my old thievish ways, and became worse and worse. . . . The robberies I have committed are so numerous, that I scarce can describe them all.

"Now all the time I was carrying on these wicked

and notorious deeds, I never once thought that I had a soul to be saved. I waited twenty weeks at York Castle, for trial, and used to go to prayers once a day, but was so very wicked, I could scarce tell one word after being at chapel. Till the time that I came on board the *Earl Grey*, I was one of the most wicked and thievish men in existence. After I came under instruction I began to reflect on my past life; sometimes I would go into my berth, and cry to the Lord to forgive my sins; at other times I would go among the wicked prisoners like myself. I continued in that state, first thinking on my soul, and then on my sinful desires, up to the day that you gave out Isaiah liii. to be committed to memory. I was called on to repeat it on the quarter-deck. I was struck with trembling and shame after I came down into my berth and reflected on it, and I thought,—if so little a matter as repeating a chapter terrifies me, what would be my state if the Lord called on me to give an account of my sins? I then began to pray to God to forgive me my sins; and I prayed till I found, by God's help, that I could leave off all evil ways and shun bad companions.

"I went on in this way till the Lord sent the first warning to us;* and then I found that nothing else would do, but to seek salvation through faith in Jesus Christ, seeing He is the only Name under heaven whereby men can be saved. After reading the "Explanation of the Lord's Prayer,"† I understood what

* The thunder storm, November 2d.
† Published by the Religious Tract Society, Paternoster-row.

to pray for, and I never knew the meaning of it before.

"I thank God for placing me under your protection, for instruction in His holy word; and I have reason to think I shall be saved, through His calling me out of darkness into His marvellous light, for my entire thoughts are on Christ, and His salvation. I have already experienced the difference between my former and my present state, for I find pleasure in reading the word of God, and attending to the promises set before me, and the encouragement to come to Christ, the bread of life, and obtain that bread without money and without price. In concluding, I beg leave to give you my thanks for showing me that there is forgiveness for the vilest of sinners, through Jesus, according to God's holy word. (Signed) "James B—."

This youth is one of the few I have ever found amongst prisoners who received Christian instruction in a Sabbath-school. Although he appeared to have resisted and forgotten that instruction, many fervent prayers had doubtless been offered for him by his teachers, which were now answered, as well as those of his pious mother.

Our next notice is of a man named Robert T—, aged *thirty-seven* years. Although he had passed through many vicissitudes, he appears to have maintained a respectable character up to a late period of his life; but after living happily for several years in the marriage state, he was brought into contact with people addicted to intemperance, by whose example he was much injured; and the work of moral devastation, appears to have been completed, by his entering the service of a master who gave his servants too liberal allowance of strong drink. It was while in a state of partial intoxication that R— T— agreed with some of his wicked associates to engage in a larcenous transaction, which brought him to prison, to conviction and to banishment. He says, "I thank the Lord, I took care of my family, so as to have my children instructed, as it was my *duty* to do; and it grieves me to leave behind me a good wife, five dear children, and a comfortable home. My dear wife has, I believe, become a Christian since I was separated from her. And I thank God, that He hath so ordered it that I should sail in the *Earl Grey*, for I can truly say I have learned more during the three months I have been favoured with kind instruction through you, than I learned in all my life before; for I have not only learned to read better, but to love my Bible, and to put my trust in that dear Saviour, whom it makes known to us, poor sinful men. I hope never to forget the solemn warnings we have had both from fire and water, and also from the death of my fellow-men. I shall have cause to bless God for ever, that I have heard the Gospel from your lips. Once I thought that my outward good conduct was enough; but I trust I have learned, that I cannot be saved without true repentance and faith in the Lord Jesus Christ. I trust in the Lord to sustain and support me. I have no strength in myself to keep me from sin, and guide me through this wicked world, and to make me a good and useful man wherever I may spend the remainder of my days. I have thought very much about you," [at this time I was suffering under an affection that threatened to prove fatal,] "and do feel for you in your present affliction. I hope the Lord will sustain you, and comfort your heart .... Please, sir, I hope you will not be offended, and will excuse my free way of writing. This letter I could not write in the *English* language myself," [he was accustomed to speak in the Welsh tongue,] "and have got a friend to write it, but every word expresses the true feelings of my mind. I conclude with wishing you every blessing both of Providence and grace; and may we meet in heaven, where we shall sin and suffer no more for ever, is the humble prayer of (Signed) "Robert T—."

This man was one of my most valuable petty officers. To a staid gait and gentle manners, he added a most quiet and amiable disposition. Amongst those around him he exerted considerable moral influence, being admirably fitted to perform the office of peacemaker, and possessing unquestionable soundness of judgment, and the power of calm and patient inquiry; he was appointed a member of my "*Court of Investigation*," in which capacity he always did his duty to my entire satisfaction, as well as that of all the people. He exhibited in a remarkable degree the meekness and gentleness of Christ, united with great firmness in the performance of his duty.

The history of Robert T— again warns all men of

the incalculable evils involved in the debasing and destructive sin of drunkenness. This unhappy man keenly felt the severity of his punishment, the most insupportable poignancy of which consisted in the consciousness that *he had brought it upon himself*, by acts which at once dishonoured God, agonized the heart of his wife, deeply injured his children, and with crimson guilt stained his own soul. For ever blessed be the Lord for that Divine Fountain in which he found cleansing and peace, and which is ever accessible to the chief of sinners, who are invited and urged to wash therein and be clean, and live in holiness for evermore.

To the Christian philanthropist and the Magistrate, the following short history of one of my men, written by himself, will suggest some important and practical thoughts:

. . . "It pleased the Lord to bring my parents to the knowledge of Himself when I was about five years old. When six, I was sent to a Sabbath-school. In 1819, the Lord visited the school I then attended, with a revival of religion; and I thank God I trust I then felt, in some degree its influence. After being a scholar about six years, I was made a teacher; and remained in that capacity many years.

"I served an apprenticeship to my dear father, as a table-fork maker and grinder. In 1827, I was married to a very prudent young woman,—an event which proved a great blessing to me; she was one of the best of women. She became the mother of six children, five boys and a girl; four of whom, I trust, are now living. Here I beg to state that the Lord called to me by the death of one of my children. Having to attend a meeting connected with the trade, I took my dear boy in my arms, and after caressing each other for awhile, I went to the meeting, but had been there a very short time only, when I received the sad news, that my dear son whom I had just embraced was nearly *scalded to death!* I made all speed to my child; whom, after suffering about thirty hours, it pleased the Lord to take to himself.

"My dear wife it was God's will often to afflict, but I never heard her complain. In 1839, it pleased the Lord to take her also to himself; and she left behind her such evidence as admits of no doubt that she is now 'with the Lord.' In losing my dear wife, I lost my best earthly friend, and my poor children lost a most kind and affectionate mother.... With grief I must now state how I forsook the living Fountain.

"First, I began to neglect *secret prayer*, and very soon after to neglect also other means of grace; and last of all, *I gave up the perusal of my Bible.* Then came trouble upon trouble; and I, trusting to my own strength, alas! alas! fell; and great was my fall.

"My trade became very bad, and I became entangled in many difficulties; and instead of returning to Christ, alas! I took to the use of intoxicating liquors. To attempt to describe my feelings at times, when returning home to my dear children, is out of the question; it is impossible. May the Lord pardon all my past sins! Oh, how thankful ought I to be that He did not then cut me off!

"During the end of 1840, and beginning of 1841, I was entirely out of employment. What I and my dear children suffered that winter, the Lord and we only know! I was willing to work at any kind of employment, but could not get a job. I applied to a certain gentleman, who gave me some labouring work to perform. I received one shilling a day for twelve hours' daily labour for the space of six weeks, and then I received sixpence in addition to my wages. I worked for this gentleman till the 24th July, when I asked him to raise my wages, and he told me he could not, as he knew I would leave him so soon as my trade mended. At this I was very much distressed, as I desired to maintain my dear family without burdening my father and mother. That night I went to rest, but my spirit was broken. I knew not what steps to take. The devil began to tempt me most dreadfully; and I, having forsaken Christ, fell, and committed the crime for which I am now most justly suffering. On July 28th I committed a robbery, was made a prisoner, for the first time in my life, and committed for trial." [Here he gives an account of a dream which appears to have impressed his mind while in prison, with views of *hell*, and of the agency of *wicked spirits;* and the dream ended with striking views of the power of Christ, and the influence of believing prayer. Awaking from his dream, he finds himself shut up in his narrow cell in York Castle.]

"I was tried, sentenced to ten years' banishment; sent back to York Castle for a short time, then removed to the Warrior Hulk, Woolwich, where I remained about ten months; and then, thank God! was, in His good Providence, put on board the *Earl Grey.*

"The Lord has here met with me in mercy; and I shall have cause to bless Him through all eternity for placing me under your care. Through your prayers and the Gospel proclaimed by you, my mind was drawn to look again to a crucified Saviour, and to grieve that by my sins I have pierced Him afresh.

"To Jesus I am now humbly looking for a full salvation. My only plea before God is,—my Saviour died to save the chief of sinners! Oh, may my future days be all devoted to his service! The Lord has often been very merciful unto me, in saving me from death. My trade being a grinder, and our stones running at a great speed, if one break, and the man is not killed, it is considered wonderful. With me *five* stones have broken, and I still live! What a mercy!

"That dreadful thunder-storm, which, by God's permission, visited us on the night of the 2d of November, has, I trust, had also the effect of awakening my soul to prayer and self-searching before the Lord. Blessed be his name for overruling all these things for my soul's good!

"Now I conclude this poor account of the life of a wretched sinner, whose only hope of present and everlasting peace and joy is in the *finished salvation* of Jesus Christ. May He be still more and more precious to your soul and mine, is the humble prayer of
(Signed) "R. R—k."

This narrative forcibly reminds individual Christians and Christian churches, of the duty they owe to their professing brethren when reduced, by whatever cause, to poverty, or when they appear to backslide from the Lord, either in heart or conduct.

CHAPTER VI.

All Christians required to promote the knowledge of Christ—Reformed prisoners employed on this principle—Prayer and zealous labour to be conjoined—Death of Edward Marlow—Christmas-day—The Author receives a poisoned wound—More are impressed—Letters of J. W—n, T. C—y, and John M‘D.

It has long appeared to me that, in addition to an admirable efficiency, there is a most striking sublimity in the very simplicity of the means appointed by the great Head of the church, for the sacred purpose of diffusing throughout the world the knowledge of His truth, and establishing His spiritual reign in the hearts of men. To no part of the economy of grace has this remark more obvious reference, than to the obligation laid upon every believer, to use his influence to the utmost in making known that "glorious Gospel of the blessed God," which, through grace, he has received for his own personal salvation. It is written, Rev. xxii. 17, "And let him that heareth say, Come." These words constitute it both the privilege and duty of every individual who has heard the joyful sound of salvation through faith in Christ, to commend to his fellow-sinners the Refuge to which he hath fled, saying unto them, by example and conversation, by the fervent prayer of faith and love, and by tender and judicious entreaty, "We are journeying to the place" —the heavenly Canaan, "of which the Lord hath said, I will give it you. Come thou with us and we will do thee good, for the Lord hath spoken good concerning Israel."* It was thus that the first disciples acted of whom we read in John i. They tell each other of the Divine Saviour they had found, and bring one another to hear from His lips the words of eternal life. It was thus that the woman of Samaria acted, on experiencing the Divine power of the Messiah's words; she instantly went and called her townsmen, saying, "Come, see a man who told me all things that ever I did; is not this the Christ? And many of the Samaritans of that city believed in Him for the saying of the woman."† It was thus that the members of the Christian church at Jerusalem acted, when driven by persecution, from that city; "they that were scattered abroad, went every where preaching the word."‡ And thus it is that every true Christian approves himself as *salt* appointed by God, to preserve from moral corruption and death all that comes under its holy influence. No encouragement, however, is given to private Christians to interfere with the office and *peculiar* duties of the scripturally-appointed minister,§ or to neglect the proper duties of their respective stations in the church or in the world. The faithful minister of Christ will rejoice to find in every one who is rescued through his ministry from the bondage of sin, a wise, praying, humble, and efficient help; and the multiplication of such *helps* will he regard as the most satisfactory evidence of the success vouchsafed

---

* Numbers x. 29. † John iv. 28—39. ‡ Acts viii. 4.
§ 1 Tim. iii.; Titus i.; Acts xx. 17, 28.

APPOINTMENT OF RELIGIOUS INSTRUCTORS. 133

by the Great Head of the church to his ministerial labours.

Although the serious attention of the great body of the people had been for some time arrested by the facts and doctrines of the Bible, and although so many had given scriptural evidence that they had received Christ, and taken up His cross; nevertheless, daily close examination proved that there still prevailed amongst us a deplorable amount of ignorance of the sacred writings, and want of a clear perception of the plan of redemption. The nature and multiplicity of my duties not permitting me to labour for the spiritual interests of the prisoners to the extent I desired, and which their circumstances required, I felt myself called upon to turn to the highest possible account the agency of those prisoners, who seemed to have received the truth in the love of it, and to be fitted by spiritual gifts and graces, for dealing solemnly, faithfully, and prudently with the understandings and consciences of their fellow-prisoners.

Accordingly, the most intelligent, spiritual, and prudent of the people, particularly of the petty officers and schoolmasters, were spoken to on this interesting and momentous matter, and one of them was appointed to every one or two messes, the members of which he engaged to consider the objects of his special care, with a view to the instruction of each in the things belonging to his present and everlasting peace. Thus the prison, to adopt the language of Dr. Chalmers, was *localized*, and not one of my people left without a spiritual instructor, who charged his own conscience with the furtherance of their best and highest interests. In communication with these spiritual monitors was my efficient "help," W. B., who was in daily and constant correspondence with me. This arrangement was made Dec. 21st, on which day, in addition to our usual morning and evening meeting, we, to the great satisfaction of the prisoners, set apart an hour for spiritual exercises, from one to two o'clock, P. M.; and this practice the people, *of their own accord*, and with great apparent seriousness and the most pleasing outward decorum, kept up to the termination of the voyage.

On the day following, the schoolmasters were assembled and solemnly addressed with reference to the spiritual state of their pupils, and were urged to take the utmost pains to instruct them in the fundamental facts and doctrines of the Bible, and the pious amongst the prisoners manifested a desire to meet together, to lift up their hearts in prayer for the outpouring of the Holy Spirit upon themselves and their fellow-sufferers: especially on such as were yet under the influence of the powers of darkness.

Dec. 22d,* we had further evidence of several being deeply impressed.

A few, who caused me painful apprehension, were solemnly and faithfully addressed as to their ignorance, folly, and danger; and means were adopted for more

* In the remainder of my narrative, circumstances induce me to quote occasionally from my rough journal, and to give dates.

efficiently advancing the education of such as had made the least progress.

In the Acts of the Apostles,* we read of "*certain lewd fellows of the baser sort*," who hindered the work of the Lord even under the ministry of the inspired Apostles. Among the prisoners in the *Earl Grey* there were one or two, to whose understandings and consciences a very faithful and strong appeal was made from the text now quoted, and I trust, through the blessing from on high, not without good effect.

Dec. 23d, besides our usual devotional exercises and examinations, the whole of the people were engaged for a considerable time in the evening, in the reading of the Scriptures, and in special prayer and praise. Our supplications had particular reference to *the promised influences of the Holy Spirit.* Those who knew the Lord were again earnestly exhorted to work while it is *day*, for the benefit of immortal souls.

It was the practice of the Apostle of the Gentiles to teach not only "publicly," but also "from house to house." The *spirit* of this apostolic practice admitted of introduction even into the internal economy of a transport. We could not indeed teach, "from house to house," but from *mess* to *mess*, and from *berth* to *berth*, we could; and those who seemed most earnestly and devoutly concerned for the instruction and salvation of the people, were exhorted to be most fervent in prayer, and strenuous and prudent in their labours; to converse quietly, unostentatiously, and in the spirit of fervent and believing prayer, with every member of

* Chap. xvii. verse 5.

the several messes assigned to their special care, so that there should not remain one man to whom the Divine plan of our redemption had not been explained, and upon whom the reception of Christ had not been closely and faithfully urged with reference to his immediate and eternal salvation.

Dec. 24th, was a solemn and impressive day. About half-past one, P. M., all those who seemed to have embraced the Gospel, or who were inquiring after salvation, assembled in the ward, to unite in earnest prayer for the still more abundant effusion of the Holy Spirit upon us all; and for the conversion to God of our fellow-sinners around us. I was able to be present; three successively conducted the devotional exercises, of whom two were prisoners; and I embraced the opportunity, to address all present from Malachi iii. 16, 17; Matt. xxi. 22; and Rev. xxi. 17; with special application to our present circumstances. The Lord, I trust, was graciously present with us.

But, alas! every scene under the sun is chequered. Edward Marlow, who served long as a soldier, and passed many years in India, is suddenly seized with a disease, most obscure as to its character, and which bids defiance to all remedies. His hours are evidently numbered, and his mind remains enveloped in thick darkness. The most anxious and prayerful effort is made to exhibit to him, in the simplest and most encouraging form, that truth, the reception of which is essential to his salvation. But he tries to cloak himself under excuses, alleging that he is "*not learned.*" It is attempted to fix two ideas in his mind; first, " *I* am a guilty sinner;" second, "*Jesus is an all-sufficient and willing Saviour!*"—Oh, how fearful is the condition of that person who *delays* to take refuge in Christ! How awfully dark is this poor man's mind! How successful are the efforts of Satan, on an unenlightened and deceitful heart, averse to the holiness of Divine truth! How long may people sit under the most affectionate and urgent calls of the Gospel, and manage effectually to exclude every ray of its saving light from their benighted souls. At every turn we are reminded of the necessity of the omnipotent influences of the Eternal Spirit, without which, every soul of man must perish in the wilful and most sinful rejection of Christ, the unspeakable gift of the Father's love. Oh! when will men take heed how they treat the strivings of the Holy Ghost?

Poor Marlow tells me he was often affected, even to distress, by what he heard from the Scriptures since he came on board; that sometimes he was under the deepest convictions and compunctions, but always managed, after much struggling, "*to get rid of serious thoughts* and *not to come to Christ.*" I continue to deal gently and truly with him; and, together with faithful and scriptural views of himself, set before him the clearest, most simple and encouraging views of Christ Jesus and His work. The poor afflicted man seems to *try* to look unto Jesus, and sometimes he seems to pray. He says he has been "a very wicked liver," and professes a *desire* to trust in the Saviour. Oh, how the dread of death distracts the mind, and gives not even one *calm* moment to perceive, understand, and believe the Gospel! Is not the work of dying, work *enough* for any hour? Should any thing be left to the hour of death, but *just to die?* Should *believing, regeneration, repentance, justification, sanctification,* and *giving evidence of our faith by the fruits of righteousness,* be left to one brief, one agitated, one distracted hour? Oh, the folly, the perversity, the wickedness of men; how incomprehensible! Salvation brought to our very door,—free, complete, most suitable,—is rejected till the last moment of life, when the soul fears to put forth her hand, and lay hold upon it, (though still in mercy urged of God to grasp it,) and so perishes in criminal unbelief!

Life is fast ebbing; the eternal world opens on his view; the dying man "*thinks he can trust in Christ for forgiveness.*" He "*thinks,*" he can; he *only* thinks he can, and has scarcely power to think, at least with calmness. The state of his heart, his real treatment of the Saviour, is known only to Him "unto whom all hearts be open, all desires known, and from whom no secrets are hid." We have no satisfactory scriptural evidence that he, by faith, laid hold on Christ—that he received the Holy Ghost, and was renewed in the spirit of his mind; and, therefore, we have no satisfactory and scriptural proof, that he was a partaker of the great salvation proclaimed in the Gospel. We cannot take a step beyond scriptural evidence; but this we know, "He that believeth on the Son hath everlasting life: and he that believeth not the Son shall not see life; but the wrath of God abideth on him."* And again, "Except a man be born again, he cannot see the kingdom of God."† And, "The tree is known by its fruit."‡ This poor man's death was traced to the physical effects of a wicked and licentious life. His case warns us to beware of indulging in any sin, and to *delay not for a moment* our believing, obedient, and thankful acceptance of Christ and of the Holy Spirit.

Dec. 25th, (Christmas-day,) was the Lord's-day: our religious exercises were all marked by solemnity. Indeed a becoming seriousness has uniformly characterized the men when assembled at *church*, and they have always made good use of their prayer-books, and generally, if not unanimously, joined in the responses. A hymn was composed by one of the prisoners, to be sung on this day; which, though it makes no pretensions as to poetry, is interesting as the song of praise of a poor convict:

A CHRISTMAS HYMN.

Awake, awake! this is the morn
On which the Lord of life was born;
Now banish slumber from your eyes,
To join the triumph of the skies.

What charming news the angels bring—
That Christ, our Prophet and our King,
Was born to save our souls from death:
Oh, blest for ever be his birth!

When Christ in human flesh appear'd,
What heav'nly music then was heard!
The valleys echoed with the sound,
And heavenly glory shone around.

---

* John iii. 36.   † John iii. 3.   ‡ Matth. xii. 33; Rev. xxi. 27.

> All glory be to God on high,
> Proclaim the seraphs through the sky;
> Good-will to men, and peace on earth,
> The angels sung at Jesus' birth.

Considerable portions of Scripture were recited by the prisoners in the afternoon. A young man who had deserted from the army, and who did not know his letters when he embarked, recited the Parable of the Ten Virgins with correctness and fluency. He now reads the New Testament very well. The whole of the Sermon on the Mount was also recited by three prisoners. Some time before the hour appointed for church, all the people assembled, of their own free will, for prayer and reading the Scriptures; and in the afternoon they voluntarily continued together for a while, and listened to W—B—, reading M'Ewen's work on the *Types*.

Conversed privately with E—d J—n, a lad aged 18 years. He decidedly appears to have received that knowledge which no man can impart to his brother; and with his simple child-like spirit I was much pleased. He is a remarkably interesting youth, and of very pleasing manners. Like many of his unhappy companions, he appears to be most completely out of his place in a transport. He states that he is the son of pious parents, and that his mother is still living. Conversed also with a man named A—A—, whose heart, I trust, Divine grace has changed. He has the appearance of a respectable country farmer. I was greatly pleased with his manners, and gratified by his spirit and conversation.

In the evening the people are addressed on Edward Marlow's death, which took place this morning, and they appear deeply impressed. They are again forcibly shown that the whole human race resolves itself into two classes—believers and unbelievers: the people of God by faith in Christ Jesus, and the children of the wicked one who live in sin and in opposition to the Divine will; and they are faithfully and affectionately urged to make their choice. A choice they *are making*, but they are entreated to make *that* choice which accords with the dictates of true wisdom, and which will receive the approbation of all eternity!

A desire to ascertain the cause of poor Marlow's death induced me to get up at daylight, which was soon after three o'clock, (being the southern Midsummer, Dec. 26th,) for the purpose of performing a *post mortem* inspection. This duty I attempted to execute in most unfavourable circumstances, and, just as I discovered that the disease was one over which medicine could have no control, I inflicted a puncture, and, as I had reason to apprehend, a poisoned wound, on my finger. A fire was lighted as speedily as possible, the wound thoroughly cauterized, and other remedies used; and with my arm in a sling I endeavoured to keep upon my legs, and proceed with my active duties, which had all along been intensely interesting.

Though suffering very severely, I managed to spend some time in prison, instructing and exhorting the people. My life was now in jeopardy, and I knew not how many hours I might be permitted to be with them. Our subjects were, the first part of Ezek.

xxxvii.; Job xxxiii. 14—24; xxxiv. 29—32, and we made seasonable reference to the Lord's special and impressive visits to us; twice by the elements,—the thunderbolt, and the waves of the sea; twice by death, —in the removal of Williams and Marlow.

A young man, accused of neglecting school, was brought before me, with whom I had most serious conversation in private. He had now been upwards of three months under instruction; and our conversation closed with this solemn and kind demand;—" Tell me, L—, what is there *now* in your character and conduct which furnishes me with matter of thanksgiving to God? For what, in you, can I retire to my cabin, and fall down on my knees, and *thank* the Lord?" The young man is perplexed; he feels in a position in which he never felt himself before; he is taken by surprise; he knows not what to say. At length he breaks silence, admits *there is nothing* in him on account of which I can praise God; and acknowledges he has been a great sinner. Christ crucified is set before him. Shortly after, this youth gave evidence of being impressed by Divine truth, attended regularly the meetings for prayer, and so conducted himself as to warrant the hope that he had taken up the cross, and set out in that way of holiness that leads through the gates into the eternal city.

Received several written communications from the prisoners respecting the state of their souls; and heard of many more being concerned about eternal things, among whom was one of my hitherto worst youngsters, J— W—n; from whom I afterwards received the following letter. It shows that "the grace of our Lord" is as " exceeding abundant " now, as in the days of Saul when he persecuted the Church; and reminds us of that gracious truth, " In Thee, the *fatherless* findeth mercy:"

"Sir,—I feel that I should make known to you how I am come to see, that I was a guilty sinner before God and man. Ever since that night of the thunderbolt, I was afraid on account of my sins, for they found me out; but by your kind treatment and good advice I was brought to see that I was in the hands of mercy, and that the blood of our Saviour Jesus Christ was sufficient to wash my guilty stains away, and to make me a new creature in Christ Jesus. I was like Paul. I was a persecutor of the people of God; but, thank God, through your teaching and the grace of God, I hope that I shall become a child of God. When I was about fourteen years of age, I first began to break out, insomuch that I left my home, and became so wicked that I lost all fear of God, and did not care for either soul or body, and I broke every commandment of God; but I hope that I have now found grace in God, through faith in our Lord Jesus Christ. I am led to see that any thing that I could do of myself is but as the spider's web.

"My father died when I was a year old, and I was only five years of age when my mother died. I was left to the mercy of God; and I hope that He has laid His hand upon me, and brought me to His one fold, and one Shepherd, Jesus Christ.

"Sir, I would like to have a little private conversation with you, if it was consistent with your will.
(Signed) "J. W—n."

From the letters of prisoners received at this time, I select two more, which may be useful in pointing out to the young the *first steps* in that downward path which led eventually to prison and a convict ship; and useful also in strengthening the faith of parents, the *fruit* of whose prayers and Christian training may be delayed, even till they are laid in the grave:

"Dear Sir,—I was born at C———, in 1810. I was favoured with pious parents, who opened their house to the preaching of the word of God. I am the son of many prayers; but, to my grief and sorrow, I have neglected to pray for myself.

"Up to the age of eighteen, I was enabled to conduct myself with propriety, and, I hope, consistently with my profession as a Christian; but my parents died, and left considerable property, which caused very much disturbance in my family, and had a very bad effect upon my mind. One trouble brought on another, and instead of carrying my griefs to the Lord, who alone could give me peace, and support me in my difficulties, I madly took to drinking, to drown my sorrows: but 'many sorrows shall be to the wicked,'— and so I found it, to my cost. I got worse every day, until I broke the laws of my country; for which I am now most justly suffering. When I was at the *Justitia* hulk, I thank God, I thought upon my ways, and took to reading the Scriptures,—but am not able to say I was turned to the Lord and in Him relied; but since I have been on board this ship, I bless God that your kind instruction has been very useful to me. I believe, through grace, my soul is saved. I desire to come to Jesus as a guilty sinner; I trust I have found peace in Christ. A little book you lent me, called 'The Two Apprentices,' was very much blessed to me. I have no other hope but in the finished work of Christ. I wish to love and serve Him, and may I enjoy His smile for ever. (Signed) T— C—."

"Sir,— . . . . My parents were pious; they did their duty to me, as parents ought to do to a son; they gave me a simple education, and instructed me in the paths of peace. My father made it his duty to see that I always attended Divine worship,—likewise school: but alas! when I grew up, I began to turn my back to my parents and their instructions.

"I was sent to a good master, a brass-founder, I stopped with him about a year; but Edinburgh, sir, you are aware, is a city where there are many temptations. I became acquainted with bad boys, left my trade, and turned a deaf ear to the many supplications of my dear parents. At last I left the peaceful roof that sheltered me from the storm, and went to sea. But I was always changeable: I left my ship after a voyage out to America, and came home once more to my parents. I saw that I had been wrong, and I complied with the wishes of my father; but, oh, sir, I am afraid to tell you!—Satan is always ready to tempt us,—I again fell into the snares of evil company. My friends disowned me; I became an outcast, and a vagabond on the face of the earth. Tired of such a life, I was resolved to leave my country; and for that purpose committed the crime for which I am exiled.

"Even after I knew my doom, I never once reflected on my state; I did not think on the God I had so often offended, till I came under your charge. The constant reading of the Scriptures, together with your kind instruction, brought me to think of my state. I considered I had a soul to save, and that it would be saved if I believed on Jesus. But when the Almighty visited us in his mercy with that thunderbolt, and also that sea we shipped, I then thought more of my situation. Ever since those visitations, my conscience tells me I am a vile wretch, unfit to do any thing for myself but to come to the Lamb of God, who taketh away the sins of the world. I hope God will give me grace to come to Him, and never to depart from Him.

"Sir, I have to return my sincere thanks for your kind instruction, and likewise for the Bible you were pleased to give me. . . . . I will ever pray to God, to direct my steps never to go out of the narrow path that leadeth to life. (Signed) John M'D—."

On the following day, Dec. 27th, my symptoms had not improved; yet I considered it my duty, and certainly my great *privilege*, to be as much as possible at my post amongst the people, but was compelled to make large use of the services of W. B., whom I now

GENERAL GOOD AND DEVOUT BEHAVIOUR. 147

released from the duties of a schoolmaster, directing him to devote his entire time and energies to the spiritual instruction of the prisoners, with the view of "winning their souls," to Christ; and the most suitable among those who appeared to have dedicated themselves to the Lord were conjoined with him in this sacred work. In the evening I was absolutely not able to attend in the prison, but was informed by one who was present, that the spontaneous meeting of the people for reading the Scriptures, mutual exhortation and prayer, was truly affecting; that the prayers presented to God for me were most affectionate and fervent; and that he never observed such a solemn silence in his life, as prevailed when W. B. was speaking to his fellow-prisoners. A great body of the prisoners appear now literally to live upon the word of the Lord and prayer; and the affectionate feelings they manifest towards me, and the deep interest they take in my recovery, are truly touching, and almost too much for my strength to bear. Oh, may all these prisoners be Christ's free men!

Dec. 28th brought me no relief from bodily suffering, which compelled me to remain in my cabin; but in the afternoon an accusation was brought, by certain persons on board, against two of my men, which compelled me, at all hazards, to go down into the prison to investigate the report. It proved entirely false; and the well-sustained evidence I received of the good behaviour of the prisoners was most satisfactory. I took the opportunity to exhort all, and especially the petty officers and school-masters, to be habitually most careful of their conduct and carriage towards every person on board—to observe strictly our standing regulations—not on any account to quit, for a moment, the portion of the decks assigned them—to perform every duty with exactness and in the spirit of the Gospel—to watch against the *appearance* of evil, and beware of every thing that *tends* to bring a blot on Christianity, or afford gratification to the great enemy of souls. The good feeling, diligence, and zeal manifested in the performance of their various duties, and, above all, the Christian seriousness which marked the spirit and deportment of a large body of the people, were in the highest degree gratifying; and though I returned to my cabin with aggravated symptoms, my mind was exceedingly soothed and encouraged.

Between two and three o'clock on the morning of Dec. 30, I awoke in great suffering, and ascertained that the most threatening inflammation surrounded my wound, which began to ascend towards the trunk. My danger could not be concealed; a fatal termination in such cases is a common occurrence, and I was warranted to regard myself as probably now drawing near to the end of my earthly pilgrimage. The circumstances in which I was placed in the *Earl Grey* were unprecedented both in my experience and knowledge; but I do not see that any good end could be answered by my entering into a detail of those circumstances. It is, however necessary to the unity of my narrative to state, that, being cut off from immediate communication with my men, I had no alternative but to direct my removal to my hospital, where a berth was instantly prepared for my reception. Here I received, night and day, the unwearied and devoted attention of the prisoners; and nothing could exceed the zeal, the good feeling, and the sleepless watchfulness with which they waited upon me. They seemed to identify my life with their own. If any thing could be more gratifying than their kindness and sympathy towards me personally, it was their manly, consistent, and admirable behaviour, without, to my knowledge, one single exception. The most fervent prayers were, I believe, with tears, offered up for my life and restoration to health, and to my post amongst my now afflicted people. Such of them as I desired to read the Scriptures to me, came to my bed-side, and their conversation and prayers were most edifying and soothing. Nothing could appear more opposite to the supposed character of a *convict ship*, than was the general aspect of the *Earl Grey*, as respects the spirit and conduct of the prisoners. I felt myself surrounded by people who feared and loved God, and were influenced by a Christian spirit; and their treatment of me was like that of the oldest, most faithful, and devoted friends. The power of the Gospel of Christ upon these men's hearts and minds was most manifest and afforded matter of earnest thanksgiving.

The petty officers and schoolmasters continued to carry on the duty in my absence, and the routine was as regularly and efficiently conducted, as if I had been mingling as usual amongst them.

Jan. 1st, 1843, was the Lord's day; and though not yet out of danger, and quite unable to conduct the religious exercises of the prisoners, I was present when they assembled below for church. W. B. read the lessons and the sermon.

After sermon, I was just able to say a few words to the people, with reference to the fearful language implied in the refusal of any of them to return to God by the believing reception of Christ: is it not this?—" I have resolved that there shall never be joy in the presence of the angels of God over *my* conversion! I have purposed that Jesus shall never see in *me* the fruit of the sore travail of his soul! It is my resolution that the ranks of Satan shall never be thinned by my going over to Immanuel, and submitting to His authority! My utmost I will do to frustrate His grace, and resist His Spirit! It is my purpose that the Divine Saviour who died upon the cross to make atonement for the sins of the world, shall never present *me* to the Father with exceeding joy! You tell me of the finished righteousness of Christ; that God is just in justifying even the most ungodly who avail themselves of that righteousness; that He is beseeching me to be reconciled to Him, and that He is long-suffering to us-ward, not willing that any of us should perish, but that we all should come to repentance, but *I have resolved* to adhere to my sins, to retain my guilt,—to abide by Satan, and to perish with him for ever!—and, more than this, I propose that my example and influence shall *continue* to be such, as are calculated to induce the greatest possible number of my fellow-transgressors to put Christianity away from them also, and with me to endure the torments of a conscience, and of felt and chosen depravity, through the ceaseless ages of eternity!" Such is the appalling language of the man who perseveres in the rejection of Christ!

In the afternoon, the people assembled for recital of Scripture: thirty are prepared to repeat Luke xv., others are learning the Sermon on the Mount, Matt. v., vi., vii. Many of my men come into the hospital, to converse with me about their souls. Oh, how does God overrule evil for good, and make even the wrath of man to praise Him; although man's evil is still man's evil; man's wrath still man's wrath; for which he must give an account unto him, who shall in righteousness judge the world by Jesus Christ, Acts xvii. 31.

There is an appearance of general concern about salvation amongst the people. A very few only seem hardened in iniquity, and even these are marvellously restrained from outward improprieties. The Spirit of grace and supplication appears to be poured out upon many, and an earnest desire to win souls to Christ. Several youths, almost mere boys, seem to have received the truth in the love of it, and are most strenuous in their endeavours to spread the gospel net, with great prudence and propriety; not presuming to teach those who are older than themselves, but giving useful information to our most experienced Christian men, respecting prisoners who are beginning to be anxious about their souls, or are held under some entanglement of the enemy, and whom these youths are most desirous to bring into contact with the truth. They act as a little body of piquets, whose watchful eyes guide the movements of our veterans in rescuing souls from the ranks of Satan.

Jan. 2nd.—Visit the people assembled in the prison, and instruct them on the fearful tendency of an *arbitrary forgiveness* of sin or of such a forgiveness as would have no respect to the requirements of law, the claims of justice, the principles of sound government, the best interests of the universe, or the character of Him who pardons. They are also shown what are the essential elements of hell, and the essential elements of heaven.

In the evening, a cloud was brought over us all. Three of the youngest prisoners were found guilty of *disobedience of orders.* Disobedience to lawful authority being one of the most heinous and destructive crimes which any man can commit, the three unhappy offenders are placed before the assembled prisoners, and their sin, after presenting fervent prayers at the throne of Divine mercy, is made the subject of a serious and earnest address. All are fervently entreated to turn this act of disobedience—an act which was not repeated during the voyage—to the best possible account, and to learn from it the character and tendency of sin, and the necessity of absolute conversion to God. " Satan must be disappointed! he must lose his object, the lawful captives must be delivered! Christ Jesus the Lord must have His *own!* Let all His children amongst us devote this night to wrestling in the most earnest prayer to God for the promised out-pouring of the Holy Spirit upon us all, for the conversion of these three offenders, and of all amongst us who have not yet returned to the Lord by the belief of the Gospel. We are to *agonize* in prayer, and, as it were, to travail in birth, like the apostle of the Gentiles, till we see Christ, the hope of glory, formed in the heart of every fellow-sinner intrusted to our care."

The unconcealable appearance of impression on the minds and hearts of the people cannot be described: dead silence, sorrowful or averted countenances, and other symptoms of sadness of heart, mark the depth of their feelings. All retire to their berths for the night.

On the following day, (Jan. 3d,) though my unfavourable symptoms had multiplied, I visited the sick amongst the prisoners, and again earnestly exhorted the assembled people from last evening's painful but most instructive text. The night appears to have been in a great measure, if not entirely, spent in earnest prayer and heart-searching—by those at least who know and love the truth. The prisoners are examined on their knowledge of justification, sanctification, and the nature and extent of the redemption of Christ. Refer, for illustration, to a prisoner placed at the bar, —he is *guilty* or *not guilty*. If found guilty, he is condemned: if not guilty, he is discharged as innocent of the crime with which he was charged. All men are found guilty before God; and are, therefore, condemned—condemned to death! On what ground can any man be discharged? not on the ground of his innocence, for he is *convicted*. He can be treated *as if he were righteous*, and discharged from the bar, on the ground only of the obedience and death of His

Divine Substitute, the Lord Jesus Christ, relied on by faith; a faith which purifies the heart, and reforms the life.

Jan. 4th.—All our meetings to-day were marked by peculiar solemnity. All who profess to be on the Lord's side, were exhorted to follow him *fully*—to beware of being ashamed of their Lord and His cross. Referred to Exod. xxxii. 26; Acts xix. 1—9, 20; Josh. xxiv. 14—28; 1 Kings xviii. 21, &c.; Acts xx. 7; v. 13; Eph. v. 11; 1 Cor. xiv. 25.

At our meeting in the afternoon, a solemn address was given on decision of Christian character;* especially directed to those who seemed to have turned to the Lord.

* Mark viii. 38; Rom. i. 16; Acts xxvii. 23.

CHAPTER VII.

Death of Abraham Button—Brief account of A. J—, J. H—, A. D—, J. J—, and others—Extracts from Journal continued—Resolution adopted by prisoners—Meetings for social prayer—Arrival at Hobart Town—Prisoners' address to the surgeon superintendent—Number of apparent conversions—Farewell address—Debarkation—Prisoner's letter.

The number of men who had been brought under conviction of sin, and whose inquiries after salvation had, to all *appearance*, issued in a believing reception of Christ, and in consistent and holy living, had now increased to *eighty-one*. These being assembled together in the prison, are, in the presence of their fellow-sufferers, briefly addressed, as now sustaining the character of professed followers of the Lord Jesus Christ. The by-standers are also addressed, and further proceedings deferred to our next meeting, in the evening, when the portion of the Scripture read, after singing a hymn, was 2 Cor. vi. and vii. 1, together with some of the texts last referred to, on the duties and privileges of Christians. All are faithfully exhorted with reference to the duties which they owe to themselves, to their Christian brethren, to the people of the world, and more immediately to God and His cause in the world.

An opportunity is taken to speak again on the subject of temperance; the evils connected with the *abuse*, frequently even with the *use* of ardent spirits; and the fearful dangers attending drunkenness, especially in the colonies. We explain the nature of the usual temperance pledge—"We agree to abstain from the use of ardent spirits, excepting for medical purposes, and to discountenance the causes and practice of intemperance;" which was submitted to them on the ensuing day, for voluntary subscription by those who care for their souls, or even desire restoration to character and to virtuous society, and who have wisdom and resolution to enter into the engagement, and set to their names. The great body of the people cheerfully enter into the proposed agreement.

This has been a day of calm and peaceful enjoyment in the soul, and truly a great day on board the *Earl Grey*. I humbly trust that the Lord Jesus is honoured this day, and His rich and free grace magnified;—that there is joy in the presence of the angels of God over these sinners, who have this day publicly professed their adherence to His cause; and that this solemn profession will be found connected with a holy and useful life, and terminate in the full enjoyment of everlasting bliss.

Jan. 5th. *Abraham Button,* a prisoner, aged 21 years, *died* this afternoon. He was a quiet, simple-minded, inoffensive, and industrious man, had the appearance of a hard-working country labourer; and was one of those prisoners who, since they embarked, appear to have been brought to repentance through faith in Christ Jesus. His views of himself and of the Saviour were truly scriptural. All fear of death had been mercifully removed by the power of the Gospel believed, and he died in the soothing enjoyment of a calm and settled peace, his purified heart evidently resting in his Saviour's love. I communicated with him as often as I was able, and was always much gratified by his happy state of mind. He had made an open declaration of his faith in Christ several weeks before his death, which seemed to affect the whole of the prisoners, those especially who watched over him during his illness; the character and spirit of whose attentions, united with the general tenor of their conversation and life, tended to evince that their own hearts were under the influence of Divine truth.

Jan. 6th, the funeral of Abraham Button took place. While I previously visited the sick, the people assembled of their own accord in the prison, for devotional exercises; and nearly the whole of them voluntarily continued in prayer until the bell tolled for the funeral, when they all repaired in a body to the upper deck. The funeral service I undertook to read myself; and on no occasion did I perform this solemn and impressive duty with more comfort in my own mind, though we were all much affected by the deceased's death, and the nature of our devotional exercises. I had the most pleasing conviction that God had taken to Himself the soul of a Christian brother, whose body we were committing to the deep, to await the morning of the resurrection—when the sea shall give up her dead, and the bodies of the saints shall be fashioned like unto the Saviour's glorious body, and made fit for an indissoluble union with the soul; that all the members of Christ, their everliving Head, may serve and enjoy God through the endless ages of eternity!

At the afternoon meeting, W— B— gives us all a very interesting and most satisfactory account of the state of *Abraham Button's* mind, both before and greater than mine; and his statements perfectly tally after he was taken ill. His opportunities of becoming intimately acquainted with the deceased were much with what came under my own observation.

The people's attention is called to those texts, which set forth the state and character of God's children, and likewise of the ungodly. Further additions are this day made to the number of those who confess Christ.

Jan. 7.—The people are again seriously addressed on the subject of temperance. *Eight* more of the prisoners avow their relinquishment of sin and Satan, and profess their devotedness to Christ and to holiness, through grace. *Ninety* of my people have now publicly avouched the Lord to be their God, and have professedly taken up the cross to follow Him fully, in His own Divine strength. They are very attentive to their duties, and seem to be under the abiding influence of the Gospel of peace. W. B. occasionally reads to the people portions from "England's Exiles."

The prisoner A— J— has been hitherto a source of great grief to me, and to the well-disposed among his companions. Nothing seemed to produce a permanent impression upon his mind. The effects of the thunder-storm had gradually died away; and although he was much alarmed when the sea fell on board of us,—awoke from his sleep in a terrible fright, and came running to me in the hospital, in almost a state of phrensy, apprehensive that the ship was going down under his feet,—yet the impression made at that time also was permitted to die away. How true it is, that no permanent or saving change can be effected in the human heart by any cause short of the almighty power of the Holy Spirit. At length, observing the prisoner T— G— one day conducting, in prayer, the devotions of his fellow-prisoners, his mind was forcibly struck; and he could not help secretly exclaiming, What! T— G— pray! Can he pray? Has T— G— come to Jesus? and is he accepted? Then why not *I?* said he to himself, and burst into tears. He continued deeply affected; and throughout the night was in a state of great concern about the safety of his soul. Two or three of the converts to Christianity spent almost the whole night with him, successively or together, praying with him, instructing him, and endeavouring to lead him to Christ, who will not *upbraid* sinners, or ungraciously cast their sins in their face (James i. 5,) when they draw near in lowly self-abasement to His feet.

One of these men acquainted me with this poor prisoner's case, begging that he might be allowed to see me; and the result of my interview with him this day, and of my inquiries concerning him is, that I dare not refuse to recognise A— J— as a man whose heart the

Lord hath touched, and disposed to bewail his past life, embrace the Saviour, and live according to His commandments, under the purifying influence of His love.

J— H—, one of my most active and efficient petty officers, a man of great natural firmness, who has been most useful to me and to his fellow-prisoners, observing every thing that may be going on both above and below decks; and whose conduct during the voyage has been most unexceptionable, communicated with me to-day on the subject of his spiritual and eternal interests; and gives evidence of being brought back to God through the faith of His dear Son. This prisoner is a very *manly* person in his disposition, habits, and carriage; and the proofs of his sincerity are peculiarly satisfactory. Oh, I trust the Lord the Spirit is performing *all* this work! If so, *all* will stand—even to the end. That which He does *not* do, will come to *naught*, and the spiritually convicted sinner will remain under an awfully increased load of guilt!

January 8th, The Lord's day.—A prayer-meeting was voluntarily held this morning, before breakfast, by all the professed followers of Christ.

A— D— and J— J— used literally to hate one another, and were perpetually betraying a disposition to quarrel when below. Observing J— amongst those who had professed to turn to the Lord, the mind of D— was arrested: he began to reason from J—'s case to his own, and thence to draw encouragement. The sight of his companion in iniquity, in the midst of those who had turned their backs on sin and Satan,

EFFECT OF A MESSMATE'S EXAMPLE.

and were enjoying happiness in the service of God, filled D— with amazement, and led him also to seek pardon, peace, and life at the foot of the cross: and now D—, as well as J—, is reckoned among the humble followers of Christ. Oh the triumphs of Divine grace! The whole mess (consisting of eight persons,) of which these two men are members, is now most happily changed in its character.

Three or four of the prisoners have on three occasions lately manifested their purpose to adhere to the service, or rather the *slavery* of Satan, by placing themselves during Divine worship as far from the sound of God's word as they can, without (as they vainly imagined) exposure to detection. These men, when it happens to blow fresh, and there is much "tumbling motion" in the ship, are observed to be most terribly frightened, and get up to the top of one of the ladders on the weather-side of the vessel, which leads from the prison to the main deck; foolishly fancying, in their state of alarm, that they are safer there than on the lower or prison deck! Oh, the folly, as well as danger of living in sin, and refusing to come to Christ for pardon and peace, which would remove the fear of death and fill the heart with holy joy!

I am told that none of the prisoners, not even the most thoughtless and depraved, ever showed the smallest disposition to absent themselves, or to skulk behind backs in the outskirts of the assembly, all the time my life was in danger.

After dinner the people assembled in the prison for recital of Scripture: but I am compelled to employ

W— B—, to occupy part of the afternoon in reading to the people from Angell James's *Young Man from Home;* a book which has deeply interested the prisoners, and has been in such constant request, that it is literally worn out. This work, and the little book called *The Two Apprentices*, appear to have been really blessed to those who have perused them.—In the evening our subject of instruction was the Prodigal's return. Luke xv.

This morning I received from three of the prisoners a written intimation of the change that has taken place in their views, and of their desire to unite with us in the service and worship of God, as His people; and this evening, my sufferings and excessive exhaustion having compelled me to retire to my cabin, I have received a note from W— B—, in which he says, with much joy of heart, that he believes " the Spirit of the Lord has been working upon many souls this day by His holy word. Since tea," he continues, "I have been beset by those who desire to have conversation on the subject of their soul's salvation. I am only sorry that I am not able to converse with every awakened soul to-night;"—alluding to his being worn out by fatigue; for he is a very delicate man, and is much affected by the spiritual work going on around him.— "In the morning I hope to be able, through the Holy Spirit's aid, to speak a word of advice and comfort to all of them. I am sure you will unite with me, and with all who are acquainted with these good tidings, in pouring out our hearts in earnest and believing prayer for the souls born of His Spirit on this holy day.

Oh, that the Lord may pour out into our souls an abundant supply of the Spirit; that we may wrestle with Him on behalf of those who appear to be anxious to know what they are to do to be saved. I believe there are *seven* or *eight*, or *more*, who are now under deep and anxious concern about the safety of their souls. —Glory to God! (Signed) W. B."

A man, named J— C—, of rather feeble intellect, seems to be under Divine teaching, and most unexpectedly to me, and almost to every body, declares his renunciation of sin, through grace, and devotedness to Christ. He has, for some time past, been diligent in reading books, calculated to make him wise unto salvation. During the first part of the voyage he was troublesome, partly from downright want of *mind;* but now he seems to possess quite "another spirit." Oh, how Christianity tends to improve all the faculties of the mind, and the affections of the heart!

All my *local labourers* continue at their posts. Our *"City Mission"* is in full operation.

Jan. 9th.—Much spiritual and anxious concern appears amongst the whole of the prisoners. From the earliest hour in the morning to the latest in the evening, private prayer-meetings are held amongst the people, while they guard against the slightest infringement of our standing rules and regulations. Several of the worst characters have renounced their former habits and manners, and appear to be under the blessed influence of the Holy Spirit. At a very early hour one morning, W— B— is aroused by hearing voices in a distant part of the prison. He feels anxious, not knowing what may be going on; leaves his berth, and creeps silently along the side of the ship towards the bows, from whence the sounds proceed. What is his astonishment to see there, three of the very worst of the prisoners, (one of them a most noted character for his wickedness, and a special cause of grief to the well-disposed,) on their knees; withdrawn to that part of the ship where there is the greatest quiet and seclusion from observation; offering up, in short and broken prayers, their deep confessions of sin, and their earnest cries for mercy,—pleading the sufferings and death of the Lord Jesus. Many of the people awakened by the sounds, stand round, in silent astonishment, to see these men so engaged. It seems to be indeed the very work of the Spirit of God in their hearts.

This afternoon we had a case of Christian discipline. A young Welshman was taken by surprise, and suffered himself to be betrayed into sin by speaking in a manner unbecoming the Christian character. He appeared very penitent, and evidently values very highly the privilege of uniting with us in spiritual exercises. He was solemnly, faithfully, and kindly admonished and "rebuked before all," as the offence was public; and he remains the object of kind and brotherly sympathy. The following texts were read on this occasion; Lev. xix. 17; 1 Tim. v. 20; Gal. vi. 1; Matth. xviii. 15—20; Luke xvii. 3, 4; James v. 19, 20; 2 Pet. ii. 1, 2; 1 Cor. v. 4; 2 Cor. ii. 7. We are to study for edification, 1 Cor. xii. xiv.

Eighteen men are this day added to the number of those who appear to have taken up the cross, and set out on pilgrimage to the Zion above! Thus the number of professed and apparently sincere followers of the Lamb amongst the prisoners, has increased to *one hundred and eight*. Oh, what hath God wrought! For ever magnified be the riches of His free and Sovereign grace!

Jan. 10th.—My continued indisposition, and urgent official, as well as professional, duties, oblige me to make much use of the services of the most pious and consistent of the prisoners. The evening meeting was exceedingly interesting and encouraging, and W— B.'s prayers most seasonable, scriptural, and consoling.

There is something in the pouring forth of the heart of a prisoner in prayer, in the midst of his fellow-prisoners, that is deeply touching and impressive. The minds of the people are evidently solemnized by the prayers of their former associates in crime—their present companions in suffering. The meeting concluded with a special prayer for the continuance of a work of grace amongst us; for the Governor of Van Diemen's Land; and for the Divine guidance of his Excellency's heart and mind in the disposal of the prisoners in the *Earl Grey*.

All assemble three times a day for reading, exposition of the Scripture, and other devotional exercises. Their private prayer-meetings are generally held before breakfast, soon after break of day. Practical and impressive instruction is, this day, drawn from Hebrews vii—x.

Jan. 11th.—At our meeting at one o'clock, P. M., the people, through M— F— P—, submitted to me a resolution, which, should it receive my approval, they had agreed to adopt, and of which the following is a copy:

"We, the undersigned, prisoners by the *Earl Grey*, have resolved, should it meet the approbation of those placed in authority over us, to lay by a portion of our earnings until we have saved the sum of TEN POUNDS sterling each, to be placed in the hands of His Excellency, the Governor of Van Diemen's Land, for transmission to the Chancellor of the Exchequer in England; as a practical expression of our sorrow for the injury we have inflicted on our country and on society, by our former irregular and illegal conduct; and, at the same time, as a small contribution which is most justly due from us, towards the defraying of those expenses to which we have most unhappily put our country and Government; and further, as a proof of the change that has taken place, during our voyage, in our character and views; as well as an intimation of our humble determination with Divine aid, to live and act, in future, as loyal and obedient subjects, and as it becomes reformed, upright, and useful members of the community."[*]

I expressed my approbation of the spirit and object of this resolution, and promised to submit it to the

[*] This document bears the signatures of *one hundred and thirty-two* of the prisoners.

consideration of his Excellency, Sir John Franklin, the Lieutenant-Governor of Van Diemen's Land.

Verily, Jesus was felt to be in the midst of us, at our evening service, according to his faithful word of promise. Never did I, at any former period of my life, receive such illustrations of the following texts, as since I embarked in the *Earl Grey:* Eph. vi. 18; Rom. viii. 26, 27; Jude 20. Observe, also, Isa. lxv. 24; Matt. xxi. 22.

We concluded with a fervent address to those who continue to put Christ away from them,—even *now,* at the end of the voyage—*now* that the hills of their new country are in sight!—the country in which they all, with perhaps one or two exceptions, are, from the unhappy choice of their past lives, destined to spend the remainder of their days! " Do you purpose to land on these shores the enemies of God, in the very act of rejecting His beloved Son, who died for you; and of resisting the Holy Spirit that seeketh to dwell in you? Do you purpose using your influence to corrupt and destroy the colony, as you have your native land?" The Gospel is again faithfully and affectionately declared to them. They are urged not to frustrate the prayers now offered in their behalf; not to live in sin and under sentence of death another hour, but *this night—this moment,* to flee to Jesus, and take refuge under the sprinkling of his atoning, peace-speaking, and purifying blood.

Jan. 13th.—The prisoners appear most anxious to make the most of their remaining days and hours on board. They very frequently select for singing, portions of the 51st Psalm. It seems well to accord with their own views and feelings.

Conversed privately this evening with two very interesting lads, about seventeen years of age, who seem very anxious about their salvation, and express their desire to follow the Lord Jesus. Conversed also with a young man who appears to have wounded the mind of a fellow-prisoner by an offensive remark. He seems truly sorry, and offers a becoming apology to the person offended; thus peace is restored, and both parties are edified.

Jan. 14th.—After morning worship I proceed to the distribution of Bibles, Testaments, and prayer-books amongst the people; in which I am assisted by my petty officers and school-masters.

The following extracts from the letter of a prisoner, afford a specimen of the value put upon these copies of the Scriptures, as well as of the change wrought in his own heart:

. . . . "Here like a penitent I stand, and here confess my sins: for the Lord has 'searched me out and found me,' Psa. cxxxix. 'Be sure your sins will find you out,' Num. xxxii. O sir! I am like the prodigal son, and like the lost sheep, and now I am found. . . . . I humbly thank you, and kind friends, for the books which they have placed under your care, to give to a sinner like me. If you had placed a large sum of money in my hands, it would not have pleased me so well as that blessed Bible which you gave me. I kindly thank you for it, and hope you will pray for me."

About noon, the *Earl Grey*, through the preserving care and boundless mercy of God, safely anchored in Hobart Town harbour.

An officer of the army, who is also a justice of the peace, came on board to visit me and joined in our social worship in the evening, when he delivered an address, in which the men appeared much interested. He specified the temptations to which they would be especially exposed in the colony; gave them seasonable advice, particularly respecting the use of intoxicating liquors, and earnestly exhorted them to become members of the Temperance Society. This officer is very much struck, and highly delighted with the appearance of the people.

After prayer and reading of the Scriptures, J— R—, my inspector of schools, rises and begs leave to address me; and in a very pathetic and appropriate speech requests my permission to read an *Address*, which he describes as the unanimous expression of the sentiments of the prisoners on board the *Earl Grey*, without one single exception. The address is as follows:

TO DR. COLIN A. BROWNING, R. N.

"Honoured Sir,—The thought of being separated from our friends casts a gloom over the mind; but to be parted from one who has taken such a deep interest in our present and eternal welfare, is peculiarly painful.

"As an officer, a gentleman, and a Christian, from the first moment you came among us in the yards of our respective hulks, your manner to us has been that of a fond and an affectionate father to his long-lost and prodigal offspring. You addressed us, though a disgrace to onr friends and our country, and degraded in our own and the public estimation, as fellow-sinners, and as subjects of God's moral government. To ensure the instruction of our minds, you daily poured on our hearts a flood of comfort and consolation, from the encouragements of the Gospel to the chief of sinners. Your fervent prayers, we hope, have been heard and answered, and your instructions applied. You clearly showed us from Scripture, and our own experience, the effects of disobedience and of a profligate life, and the connexion that subsists between sin and suffering.

"By your unwearied exertions, the word of God, which comparatively few could then read, is now no longer a sealed book to any one of us. Self-government, and an implicit compliance with the lawful injunctions of our superiors, have been inculcated and strongly recommended to our observance. Nor have our social and relative duties been overlooked or forgotten, in the midst of your multifarious avocations; for whatsoever things are true, honest, pure, lovely, and of good report, have been set before us, and impressed upon our minds.

"Confessing our unworthiness before God, we desire with heart-felt gratitude to bless Him for preserving us from the fury of the thunder-bolt, the storm and the tempest; from the rage of conflicting elements, and the power of disease: but in an especial manner, we praise Him for making known to us by His word and Spirit the way of everlasting life, through the mediation of His dear Son, our only hope and Redeemer; and as we know your aversion to every thing like adulation, your conviction that all spiritual illumination and improvement are alone effected by the Eternal Spirit—are fully aware of the *dread* with which you regard the very thought of referring to any creature that which is to be wholly attributed to the Almighty power of the Holy Ghost—we would, while we thank God for your instrumentality, desire to unite with you in rendering to Him all the glory of all the saving work, which He hath been graciously pleased to accomplish in any of our hearts during our passage from England to these colonies.

"We would congratulate you on your recovery from your late illness and imminent danger, and pray to God to perfect, in His goodness, your health, and to comfort your soul with the joys of His Holy Spirit.

"We beg to express our warmest thanks for your patient, careful, and successful attention to the sick: for your earnest efforts to instruct our minds, to enlarge our understandings, to extend our knowledge, to improve our morals, and to persuade us at all times, particularly during our present unfortunate situation, to be most attentive to our respective duties. For these, and for every other act of kindness experienced at your hands, we feel sincerely grateful: and deplore that any one of us should, at any time, have caused to your mind the slightest uneasiness; or should have done or said any thing to meet your disapprobation, or demand your censure.

"Whilst we lament our misconduct and misfortunes, we confess the justness of our sentence, and beg leave to profess our attachment and loyalty to our Sovereign, and attachment to her Government; our resolution, by a willing submission to the laws of her representative in the colonies whither we are bound, to approve ourselves as reformed from our vices and follies; and we earnestly implore that Divine grace may enable us to submit in a proper form, to do all things as unto Christ Jesus.

"We also beg to acknowledge the kindness of the Admiralty in providing for our wants and comforts on our way hither.

"Honoured Sir, we cannot take our last leave of you without feeling a deep sense of sorrow, that our crimes were the cause of our meeting, and must also be the cause of separation, and that to opposite sides of the world, in all human probability, never to meet more on this side the grave! Oh, may we all, through rich and free grace, meet in heaven!

"We beg to be affectionately remembered to the kind and Christian friends and benevolent societies, who aided you in making so careful and liberal a provision for our spiritual wants. May you all partake largely of the blessings, the peace, and the joys of the Holy Ghost in Christ Jesus: to whose care we commit you, and wish you, with all our hearts, a safe and happy return to the bosom of your beloved family, and to your friends!

"And that the peace of God may rest and abide on you all, now and for evermore, is the unanimous and earnest prayer of us all; in whose name, and by whose permission, I am,

"Honoured Sir, your most obliged,
"Most dutiful, and obedient Servant,
(Signed) "J—R—,
"Inspector of Schools.

Submitted on board the Earl Grey, *in the Harbour of Hobart Town, January* 14*th,* 1843.

The address I received as containing an expression of the sentiments and feelings of the prisoners in reference to their sovereign the Queen; her Majesty's representative in the colony; the Lords Commissioners of the Admiralty; the laws under which they live; and to those benevolent societies and friends in London, Brighton, and other places, who had so liberally contributed the means for furthering their intellectual and spiritual improvement, and securing their highest interests. In this address I trace the power of Christianity, and regard it as a tribute of praise to God, the giver of all good, and not at all to *me*, who am but an imperfect "earthen vessel," of which he is graciously pleased to make use, for conveying to those men His written word, which is effectual through the Spirit of truth alone, unto the present and everlasting salvation of their souls.

The number of prisoners on board the *Earl Grey* who have given in to me their names as professed disciples of Christ, and are observed to regulate their temper and speech, their spirit and behaviour, according to the requirements of the Gospel, now amounts to *one hundred and fourteen;* exclusive of Abraham Button, who is believed to have entered into the joy of His Lord.

The personal inspection of the prisoners in the usual way, and by the proper authorities, commenced on the morning of the 17th, and closed on the 19th. The registrar expressed much pleasure at the appearance and answers of the men; and observed how striking were the effects produced on the minds, the countenance, and carriage of men, by even a few months' scriptural instruction and sound moral discipline.

Our usual routine was conducted as regularly as the state of my health and our new engagements would allow. The examination of the schools was finally closed, and the people's progress ascertained and recorded. On the evening of the 16th, they assembled to receive from me their *farewell address*,* and to worship God together for the last time on board the *Earl Grey.*

Our last songs of praise were *Psalm* li.:

> "Have mercy, Lord, on me,
> As thou wert ever kind;"

And *Cowper's* hymn:

> "There is a fountain fill'd with blood,
> Drawn from Immanuel's veins:
> And sinners plunged beneath that flood
> Lose all their guilty stains."

At three o'clock on the morning of Jan. 20th, 1843,

* Appendix.

the boats came alongside agreeably to previous intimation, when the debarkation immediately commenced, and was speedily and orderly conducted, in the most perfect *silence*.

At the hour and place appointed, I made an effort to attend; when His Excellency, Sir John Franklin, inspected and addressed the prisoners, drawn up in open square, and spoke in high terms of approbation of their appearance, and their behaviour on board the *Earl Grey:* he endeavoured to impress their minds with just views of the advantages they had enjoyed with respect to instruction and discipline during the voyage; and assured them that their future conduct would be expected to be in unison with the privileges they had possessed on board the *Earl Grey.*

It requires a particular knowledge of the circumstances under which the prisoners are about to be placed on shore, to enable the reader to contrast them with those from which they are now removed for ever, and information on this point I cannot attempt to supply in this place.* For the present I would only observe, that it is perhaps impossible for us to conceive the feelings our prisoners experienced under the immediate prospect of landing, and when they went over the ship's side, and actually set their feet, for the first time, on the penal shores of Tasmania.

For a period of four months they had been under

---

* A letter, in the Appendix, from W—B—, a convict often referred to in these pages as being a valuable assistant to me among his fellow-prisoners, will give some idea of those circumstances. It was written on the expiration of his two years' "probation" in the colony.

the constant influence of scriptural instruction and prayer, and of a system of intellectual and moral government, founded on the grand principles of Christianity, and in unison with its spirit and precepts. They had all been eye-witnesses of the blessed effects which the knowledge, faith, and love of Christ are, under the power of the Eternal Spirit, able to produce; and these effects many of them had experienced to the praise and glory of God. If they follow the instruction they have received, they will prove holy and useful men, wise to win souls to Jesus and to heaven, by conversation, example, and prayer, and will be kept by the power of God unto the everlasting kingdom of their Lord and Saviour Jesus Christ; but it will not be manifest till that day when God shall take account of His people, how many souls on board the *Earl Grey* were *"born again"—born of the Word and Spirit of God.*

This chapter I shall close with extracts from a letter, which one of the prisoners put into my hands, as he was about to step over the ship's side into one of the boats appointed to convey him and his companions to the shore. He appears to have availed himself of the light of the midnight lamp, and to have occupied his last hours on board, (which he was neither able nor disposed to give unto sleep,) in attempting to give utterance to a heart which was too full for utterance, and whose emotions must be far beyond the sympathies of those who have not felt the plague of their own hearts, nor experienced the sweet influence of pardoning love:

* * * * * * * "Allow me to thank you most sincerely for every expression of kindness I have received from you. I acknowledge with grateful love to the ever-blessed God, that to Him alone belongs the glory and the praise for every new-covenant blessing bestowed upon the undeserving and the guilty, such as we poor sinners are, through whatever channel He may be pleased to convey His precious and free gifts, the tokens of His everlasting and unchanging love: yet I must thank you for all the kind and anxious care you have exercised towards *us all*, and towards *myself*, as an individual. It might have been with us as with many poor men in the like situation with ourselves, to have 'no man that would naturally care for our state,' as God's creatures, and as offenders against His holy laws. But thanks be to the Lord for the manifestation of His abundant goodness! Oh, sir, if I know my heart at all, I feel that it overflows, as it were, this night with sincere gratitude and love to my Lord and your Lord, to my Father and your Father, for all His goodness to my soul and body, and to us all, from the time we first stepped upon the decks of this highly-favoured ship.

"What shall I render unto the Lord for having made you the instrument of good to my soul, and to the souls of many of my poor dear companions in affliction! I am sure, dear kind friend of us poor convicts, your heart will respond, we shall bless and praise the Lord for ever!

"It is midnight now, and I feel that I could, did prudence not whisper, like Paul and Silas, break out into a song to my Redeemer, upon taking a retrospective view of all the Lord's mercy and goodness which have followed us through our lives, and especially during our voyage .... I felt, though nearly heart-broken by the thought of parting from my wife and child,—I felt, when in the hulk, such a strong desire to sail in this ship as nothing could repress, and I left no stone unturned to accomplish my object, so far as I was concerned, though very ill. But I see now, without abating aught from my sin and guilt, and moral responsibility, God would have it so. He intended good; He had thoughts of peace and not of evil towards me, a *then* careless creature.

"I bless and adore Him for His providential dealings with me. I thank Him,—oh! I do indeed thank Him, this night, that He brought me on board this ship! I cannot tell what He has done for me, through your faithful and affectionate instrumentality. But He has brought me low at His footstool to exalt me in the righteousness of the holy Jesus, who is very precious to my soul: and in His dear name I can rejoice, some days, all the day long. Oh, sir, I believe that through the grace of our Lord Jesus Christ you and I, and many of my dear fellow-men here, will be saved, and when we get to heaven, salvation will be the subject of our praise:

'Then shall we sing more sweet, more loud,
And Christ shall be our song!'

"May the Lord make and keep me very humble, and make and keep me faithful unto death! I need not remind *you* that I have no strength to resist sin and gladly to follow my Lord, bearing His cross, but what I derive from our exalted and ever-blessed Lord himself. I *feel* it! Oh, my soul longs to love Him more;—I long to be made useful to poor sinners! Oh, that I may have the opportunity! I can do it in one way, I know, by showing forth the Saviour's praise and power to save, in my life and walk, spirit and temper. The Lord open doors for me to speak to my fellow-sinners of Jesus and His great salvation; The Lord grant me wisdom and a sound judgment, and a warm heart, and an enlightened mind!

"Oh, sir, pray for me,—I will pray for you! I cannot forget you and all your kindness, and the kindness of your and our kind friends in England, who have taken so much interest in our welfare. Oh, do tell them, to the honour of our Lord, that one poor wandering sheep has been brought to the Good Shepherd who laid down His life for the sheep, He loved them so dearly! . . . I hope to meet with you, kind sir, where Jesus is; and it will be heaven where He is . . . . Oh, I feel a heaven in my soul when He dwells in me by faith, and visits me with His love; and He will never leave me:—He cannot—for He is formed in my heart the hope of glory: I dare not doubt it! Blessed be God there are many more beside me! The Lord has His own sheep amongst us;—and now we must part! I feel the smart. Blessed be that dear uniting love that binds us together!

"May God preserve you homewards, and restore you to your family in health and safety! I have been very much comforted by these words, as I have thought of you leaving us—the precious words of Jesus, which discover His relation to His believing people, and remind them of His never-ceasing care for them,—'My Father and your Father; my God and your God!' I have been reading the twentieth chapter of the Acts, and found great benefit. . . . . Excuse me in taking so much liberty as I have, in addressing to you this short letter before I quit the *Earl Grey*. Farewell."

. . . .   * * * * * *

CHAPTER VIII.

Concluding statements—Letter from Inspector of Schools—Summary of apparent good accomplished—Extract from a prisoner's letter, after he had been some time in the colony.

In perusing the foregoing narrative, the reader cannot fail to be struck with the quiet, orderly, and superior behaviour of the prisoners, the punctuality and cheerfulness with which they performed the duties involved in our daily routine, and especially with the diligence and zeal with which they attended to the great and important business of their education. It will be observed that we had no infliction of corporal punishment; a mode of dealing, at least with adult offenders, which generally tends but to debase, and harden, and to extinguish every remaining spark of virtue, self-respect, and manliness of feeling. It will be seen that the prisoners in the *Earl Grey* were governed by daily Christian instruction, accompanied with fervent prayer, and by uniformly kind and manly treatment,—that they were ruled by a consistent discipline, which uniformly required a close and punctual observance of all established regulations; a prompt, cheerful, and courteous obedience, given on right principles, to every lawful command; a becoming and respectful carriage; and the habitual use of correct and irreproachable language in all their communications with each other, and with all men. Thus we have an additional illustration of the soundness of the scheme of instruction and moral discipline which had been framed during my former voyages, and which has been detailed in another work.

"The *entire management*, as well as the medical treatment of the convicts," is very wisely, and indeed, considering that he is engaged on *naval service*, is necessarily intrusted to " the surgeon-superintendent," the only naval officer on board, who is also held responsible for the care and expenditure of Her Majesty's stores; is commanded " to issue such rules and regulations for the promotion of good order on the part of the convicts, as he may judge proper, inserting copies thereof in his Journal;" and " to appoint from among the convicts in health, those whom he may think most fit and trustworthy to act as attendants on the sick." "As it is highly desirable to keep the minds of the convicts as constantly and usefully employed as possible, he is to exert his best endeavours to establish schools, under such regulations as circumstances will permit;" is " to read the Church Service every Sunday to the convicts . . . . and also a Sermon ;" and, finally, is required *"to use every possible means to promote a religious and moral disposition in the convicts."* The authority with which the surgeon-superintendent is thus invested, and the instructions which he is required to carry into effect, fully and distinctly determine his position in the ship, at the same time that they afford the most gratifying proof of the interest with which the Admiralty regards the convicts, and the soundness of the views entertained of their condition and moral wants. Nevertheless I had to encounter obstructions to the performance of my duty in the *Earl Grey* which were comparatively unknown to my former experience; and some important provisions of the system of management already referred to, were thus rendered unavailable, and its working less efficient, and far more trying to my mind and health, than on any former voyage.* Still, as already hinted, its character was fully sustained, and my confidence in its soundness and practicability strongly confirmed.

The twenty-four schools into which the whole of the prisoners were classified, were kept in active and regular operation till nearly the end of the voyage, when some changes were made, more effectually to help forward those individuals who were still incapable of reading the New Testament with ease and comfort. The patient diligence of the teachers, and persevering application of the pupils, were most gratifying; and the active and untiring zeal of my Inspector of Schools excited my admiration. To him, to W— B—, to my chief Captain, to the other Petty officers and Schoolmasters, and to many who were not called to fill office, I have cause to feel most grateful: and it will be an unhappy day for me when I find myself capable of forgetting them and their exiled associates at the throne of grace.

* Measures have been wisely adopted to prevent, in future, any such unwarranted interference with the duties of the Surgeon-Superintendent as that to which allusion has here been made.

My monthly examination of the schools took place in the manner mentioned in "England's Exiles;" but the formation of a Board of Examiners at the termination of the voyage, as on former occasions, to wind up by a general examination, and award prizes, was, in the *Earl Grey,* morally impossible. The duty was therefore executed by myself, assisted by the most fit and intelligent of my petty officers and schoolmasters.

A Table, showing the result of our final examination will be found in the Appendix; it presents, also, a view of the state of education in my other ships. The number taught to write in the *Earl Grey* was unusually small, and for this reason:—the number who, when they embarked, were unable to read, was very considerable, and a great many of them got on very slowly, and required extra attention. I could not, therefore, spare my schoolmasters, either to teach or learn to write. It was far more important that the whole of the people should be taught to read the Bible, than that either few or many of them should be taught to write. Those who desire to learn to write may do so in the colony; but if a prisoner land unable to read the sacred Scriptures, the probability is that he will *never* learn.

After the statements made in the foregoing pages, it is unnecessary to add many words with reference to the amount of good actually or apparently accomplished, through the Divine blessing, during our voyage. The whole of the prisoners were, on landing, with one exception, able to read the Holy Scriptures; and, with

SUMMARY OF APPARENT GOOD ACCOMPLISHED. 185

two exceptions, they all landed in the possession of a Bible or Testament, and other valuable and instructive books: most of them received also a Prayer book.

Even those who gave no decided evidence that they had received the truth in the love of it, received, nevertheless, no inconsiderable benefit from the system of instruction and discipline followed out during the voyage; and though they may have hitherto, in their unbelief, put away from them the salvation of the Gospel, and thus increased their guilt and danger, yet the instruction they have received may, at some future time, either in health or sickness, be made effectual through grace to their conversion to God.

The great body of the prisoners gave unequivocal evidence of improvement, both intellectual and moral. Their behaviour towards each other, and towards all on board, was highly satisfactory. Nearly all of them had, in some degree, acquired a habit of application and the love of useful knowledge. They became thoughtful, learned to command their temper, to be obliging and courteous, and, generally speaking, conducted themselves in a manner that would have done credit to any portion of the labouring community of England. With scarcely an exception, their conversation was remarkably correct and manly; only on one or two occasions, during the whole voyage, did I hear an improper expression proceed from their lips: and I hesitate not to say, that I should rejoice to see every little community of men, whether at sea or on shore, characterized by a similar tone of decorum.

With reference to those men [114 in number,] whose

enmity to the Gospel appeared to have been subdued —who professed to take up the cross and to follow Christ, and whose temper and conduct, conversation, tastes, and habits, while on board, tallied with their profession; we dare not doubt their convictions of sin, their persuasion that in the Lord Jesus alone they had pardon and life; that they derived peace and consolation from the truth which they appeared to believe, and that by that truth their spirit and conduct were influenced; but to which of the classes specified in Matt. xiii. they positively belonged, it is not for us to say: "They shall be known by their fruit."

They had no encouragement to act the part of the hypocrite; quite the reverse. Of such unworthy and perilous conduct they were constantly warned to beware, and were faithfully shown that the course of the hypocrite only involves him in greater guilt and wretchedness, and that his hope must perish for ever! But whatever may be said of the sincerity or insincerity of any of the prisoners, in their profession of faith in Christ, and of obedience to Him, *they must stand by the decision of their lives, and of the great day.*

Here it ought to be stated, that I never report a prisoner as a reformed character unless his spirit and conduct, and experience of the power of Divine truth, correspond, as far as can be perceived, with the records and requirements of the sacred Scriptures. Were the temper and behaviour of some people, esteemed respectable, who make a great profession of Christianity, and are regarded by many as Christians, to be transferred to one of my convicts, that convict

EFFECTS OF THE PROBATION SYSTEM. 187

I could not conscientiously report as being a reformed man.

It has been hinted that the prisoners, on debarking from the *Earl Grey*, were placed in circumstances most unfavourable to the furtherance of their moral and spiritual improvement.

The Probation system which has been for several years in operation in Tasmania, places convicts in masses of 300 or 400. And when we remember the lamentable paucity of faithful labourers in the Gospel in our Penal Colonies, the extreme difficulty, if not impossibility, of obtaining pious and suitable men to fill responsible situations at Probation Stations; the character and habits of a vast majority of convicts, and their corrupting influence, when not placed under an efficient system of scriptural instruction and moral discipline, we shall not be surprised if many of the prisoners by the *Earl Grey*, even of those who appeared to have been reformed, should be again seduced for a time into sin, and subjected to punishment. In all circumstances the people of God need to be upheld by a Divine power. Severed from Christ, (John xv. 4, 5,) they can do nothing. But there are *special circumstances* in which they stand in need of *special grace;* and such are the circumstances in which the prisoners are now placed. It is indeed difficult to imagine any position under the sun in which a Christian can more urgently need the never-ceasing watchfulness and care of the Good Shepherd. The preservation of even an *advanced* Christian in such circumstances would strikingly illustrate the power of Divine grace.

Little, however, can be learned from the official reports of our prisoners under the Probation system, which can lead to any just and satisfactory conclusion respecting the steadfastness with which they adhere to the principles and requirements of Christianity. This they will strive to do in whatever circumstances they are even now placed, if they cleave to Christ as His true and humble followers; but when their probation servitude is finished, and, in virtue of their " Probation Pass," they have found their way into the employ of a godly and consistent master, they may endeavour, with increased probability of success, to carry their instruction into practice, and to evince the genuineness of their faith by the scriptural correctness of their lives.

We can now only leave them in the Lord's hands, bear them on our hearts at the throne of Divine mercy, and implore the Great Shepherd of the sheep to take care of them, and to raise up spiritual and faithful men, who may lead them into a closer and more influential acquaintance with the blessed Saviour in the cheerful and habitual obedience of faith and love. When we commend to God's fatherly goodness " *all* those who are *anyways afflicted* or *distressed,* in mind, body, or estate;" and when we implore the Lord "to show his pity upon all *prisoners* and *captives;*" let us have a special regard to all despised and unhappy *convicts,* whether men or women; who should ever be the subjects of the most earnest and believing prayer.

I am fully aware of the extent to which there pre-

THE GOSPEL REACHES TO CONVICTS. 189

vails a chilling, heartless, proud, and ignorant skepticism with reference to the conversion of a convict. But are the word and Spirit of God omnipotent? If the atonement and finished righteousness of the Messiah availed for the pardon and salvation of a Saul of Tarsus, a condemned malefactor, an Onesimus, of many even of the depraved Corinthians, and of the betrayers and murderers of the Prince of Life,*—shall they not avail for the forgiveness, purification, and life of a *Convict*—of *every* convict who believes in Christ, and honestly submits to his authority? Why should not He who died on the cross to ransom convicts, experience the promised satisfaction in presenting them to the Father with exceeding joy?

It would materially aid us in forming a just estimate of that unhappy and degraded portion of the community, and in cherishing becoming sympathy towards them, were we to think more correctly of the character and parentage of the whole human race. What epithets should we hear applied to the first offending human pair, were they spoken of as certain persons speak of modern convicts? They were united in an act of gross *disobedience,* in the perpetration of a *theft*—of a base, ungrateful *robbery,* a most aggravated *breach of trust!* Were they not detected, brought to justice, arraigned at the bar of their omniscient, just, and merciful Judge? and were they not *convicted,* and *condemned to death?* They were *reprieved,* it is true, and a full, free, and *consistent* par-

---

* Luke xxiii. 32—43; Acts viii. ix.; Gal. i. 23; 1 Tim. i.; Philemon; 1 Cor. vi. 9—11; Acts ii. 37—41; vii. 51—53.

don was provided for them; nevertheless, it was necessary that they should be *banished*—banished from their first happy residence, and sent forth into the wide, wild, and unsubdued world, doomed, by hard labour and the sweat of their brow, to eat their bread, until the earth in which they toiled for their subsistence, should receive their sinful and weary dust, in pursuance of the sentence so justly passed upon them.—(Gen. iii.)

When we speak of convicts, lament over their folly, and condemn their crimes, let us remember the history of *Eden;* let that history duly affect our hearts; let us bear in mind, also, how closely our conduct and character resemble those of the pair in whose fall we are so fearfully interested; let us recollect, moreover, that in all the rich, free, and covenant provision contained in Gen. iii. 15, the whole of mankind are most deeply concerned; and that they are, without exception, invited and required to lay hold of all that provision, for present pardon and peace, for holiness of heart and conduct, and for everlasting life and glory.

When prisoners on board a convict ship write to their relatives and friends, they send in their letters unsealed to the surgeon-superintendent, who—having thus had the opportunity to examine their contents, should he deem it necessary—seals, and despatches them.

On our arrival in the colony, the prisoners in the

CHARACTER OF PRISONERS' LETTERS. 191

Earl Grey expressed to me a strong desire to write to their relations. I accordingly supplied them with paper; and their letters, as usual, were forwarded to me. Although their number was very considerable, I was induced to glance at their contents, for the purpose of observing what subjects had been selected, in addressing friends, from whom, in most cases, the writers were separated for ever; and having good reason to hope, that most of these letters were written out of the abundance of their heart, their character was certainly most gratifying. With very few exceptions they were *impressive sermons*, whether long or short. They recounted the mercies of God vouchsafed to all on board; referred to the power of the thunderbolt, and of the waves of the sea, as experienced by the prisoners during the voyage; acknowledged their sin and need of a Saviour; set forth Christ as the only refuge of the guilty and the lost; and urged the relations and friends not to delay, but to flee to the blood of the cross for pardon and life, adding suitable exhortations on reading the Bible, the observance of the Sabbath-day, avoiding improper companions, and so forth. These letters reaching England, would, of course, be scattered over the country, among that class of the community to which the writers belong, and, with the Divine blessing, were calculated to enforce the importance of spiritual and eternal things, and of turning to the Lord by the reception of His Son Jesus Christ.

From none of the letters to which I refer did I make any extracts. But from one which was written some time after our arrival in the colony, to a near relative in England, I am induced, considering that I can do so warrantably, to make a long citation; which will prove the more acceptable to the reader, because it was not written under the remotest apprehension that it would ever meet the eye of the public. It will be in keeping, however, with the spirit which the writer evinced while on board the transport, and afterwards in the colony, if we use his letter to promote the cause of His Lord and Saviour more widely than he had contemplated. It was written at a Probation Station, at a considerable distance from Hobart, and was forwarded through the proper channel for transmission home. The extract is as follows:

" My dear,—Thanks to the Lord, I once more am permitted to write to you in the enjoyment of excellent health, though in a foreign land, and *in bondage, the desert of crime;* a fact which I wish ever to bear upon my mind, and which, with the Divine blessing, tends to humble me, and render me comparatively contented in my present situation.

" * * * I have found the Scripture declaration true, that I have a desperately wicked and deceitful heart, out of which has proceeded all that wickedness which man, or Satan, or my own conscience charges upon me, which to the Divine Being must appear exceedingly sinful, and must have sunk me to the lowest depth of misery here and hereafter, but for the hand of mercy bearing me up, but for that Sinner's Friend who bled upon the cross, that the vilest of the vile might have life, and might have it more abundantly; but though man may deem me, and that *justly*, a very scandal and curse to the earth, yet there is, I find, in God's word, one infallible rule by which I can judge of myself; viz.,—'They that are Christ's have crucified the flesh with the affections and lusts.' I trust I really do hate sin and love holiness. It makes my heart bleed to think what a *rebel* I have been, although *I am but a worm!* I am at times, I confess, rather dejected, when I think what distress I have brought, especially upon you, dear ——, and sweet child, and upon a number of dear relations and friends who loved me, and who, may I yet indulge the fond hope, still love me, though now an *exile*. Beloved friends, next to the deepest wound I feel in my heart,—the remembrance of my base ingratitude to God my Saviour, who had always been doing me good—(and, oh! may I always while I live feel its smart, rather than do such great evil again towards the Lord!)— next to this, I say, is the remembrance of the injury I have inflicted upon *you*. What I have passed through *personally*, is but a trifle to me: the sorrow I have caused *you* is my greatest grief. But I hope you pray for me. Your Saviour prayed for his bitterest enemies. So do as He did; bear me—all of you—upon your hearts before the Lord.

"I am surrounded by very wicked men; but the Lord has kept me, and will still keep the soul that trusts in Him. There are a few, I believe, who fear His name, in this notoriously wicked colony. I have here with me some of my companions who came over with me in the *Earl Grey*, to whom the instructions they received from our dear friend, Dr. Browning, the surgeon-superintendent, were blessed. I believe they are *Christians*. They are walking in the fear of the Lord, and in the comfort of the Holy Spirit. We often speak one to another of His great goodness to such bad men as we have been: and it is good thus to converse. Means of grace are not so plentiful with us, as they once were, and as you have them. Oh! my dear ——, do prize them; and tell any, who you think undervalue or neglect them, to be diligent, or they may be deprived of them, and it will pierce them then, to think of former misimprovements.—*I feel it! I do indeed feel it!*

"My dear ——, the time will arrive when, if it please God, we shall have a prospect of meeting again," [alas, a feeble prospect!*] "At present, let us wait, and put our confidence in the Lord, who causeth all things to work together for good to those who love Him: 'Be still, and know that I am God.' May He grant us patience and submission to His will! I trust my friends will not disown me. An over-anxious desire to increase my master's connexion led me into company, which brought on habits of drinking and 'treating,' and led to my ruin; and, being heedless, like those at the 'Slough of Despond,' I fell in. Oh, that my fall may be a warning to all who know me! Oh, that I could restore to one of the best of masters, what I wasted of his property in profligacy! But I

* It is supposed that the proportion of convicts who return from the Penal Colonies to great Britain and Ireland, is about *one in a hundred*.

am content to suffer this banishment; and on my own part this is the lightest of what I do suffer: I feel that I deserve ten times more. Tell Mr. ——, you have heard from his unworthy servant. I hope he is prospering, and that he will never give another journeyman the liberty he gave me. I say not these things to extenuate my guilt. Tell my dear —— to be a father to my dear child as much as he can, and the Lord will not forget his labour of love.

"Weak and prone to err, and constantly in the midst of the *grossest and most terrible wickedness*, I often tremble, knowing that I possess the elements of all that is evil in my own breast, which, did not grace prevent, would take fire, and then I should be capable of doing all that is soul-destructive: yea, which would involve soul and body in wretchedness and ruin for ever! God be thanked, He has hitherto helped me; and, though beset with snares, still I stand a monument of His mercy; and,

> 'How can I sink with such a Prop,
> Which bears the world and all things up?'

"Dearest ——, my imagination takes wing, and carries me 18,000 miles across the great sea, and places me by your side in your own humble dwelling. The first thing that rises in my mind is, How is it with your soul's concerns? are the consolations of God small with you? Your health,—the health of my child—the manner in which you get your living,—the welfare of all my dear friends and relations,—are all questions I should propose, and are important; but my great concern is to know as to the health of your precious and immortal soul. The love of Christ is to the humble penitent the never-failing source of true comfort. Nothing else but the Gospel of Christ received into the heart by faith can give us a happiness that will remain uninjured by all the changing scenes of this changing life—that will enable us to rise above the trials and troubles of this world. This happiness alone is built on the true Foundation, and it will abide for ever! It will not deceive us nor desert us in the time of need. Blessed be God! I find it so. I trust *you* do; I cannot wish you a greater blessing. In difficulties and distresses this source of happiness will be our refuge and consolation, will outlive the ruins of a dissolving world, and our happiness will flourish through eternal ages. However tried, persecuted, afflicted, tormented we may be, if our souls are under the protection of Jesus, nothing can hurt them. His peace, you know, my dear ——, is not to be destroyed by the varying circumstances of life. Peace reigns in the heart, where the powers of man cannot reach; it cannot fail us, it is fixed on the Rock of Ages, and will last for ever! . . .

"'To my deep regret (and I attribute my downfall to this cause,) I was not diligent in the use of all the means of grace, especially watchfulness and prayer, and have been wisely permitted to feel and to suffer the sure consequences of my own conduct. Once more, —it may be for the last time,—let me entreat all who profess to believe in, and follow Christ, to value private and public means of grace. Though there is an inexhaustible fulness of grace and blessing treasured up in Christ for all who hunger and thirst after righteousness, yet we often, like Hagar in the wilderness, sit weeping near the well of consolation, and will not lift up our eyes to see, nor raise our hands to receive from the Fountain of Life the waters of comfort, to the joy and refreshing of our souls. . . . May you, dear ——, draw from Him by faith, who is the Fount of every blessing, daily supplies; and the water He will give you shall be in you a well of water, springing up unto everlasting life. So prays your truly affectionate,   "* * *   * * * * *."

It is impossible to tell with what trying severity transportation, though rendered by Divine grace subservient to the soul's everlasting welfare, operates on all convicts, and especially upon such men as the writer of the above letter,—a letter which is calculated at once to show the sustaining power of vital Christianity under such an overwhelming and agonizing chastisement, and to warn every man and woman in Great Britain and Ireland against violating in any way the laws of the land, and thus *voluntarily* subjecting themselves to a punishment, the nature and tendency of which so few persons seem fully to understand, but which is, in every respect, so terrible,—so likely, in ordinary circumstances, to prove disastrous to the soul, that it ought ever to be regarded with the utmost dread!

APPENDIX.

FIRST ADDRESS TO THE PRISONERS IMMEDIATELY ON THEIR EM-
BARKATION, AND BEFORE THEY ARE PERMITTED TO QUIT THE
QUARTER-DECK.

This day commences a new era in your existence. The moment you set your feet on the decks you now occupy, you came under the *operation*, and, I trust, will speedily come under the *influence*, of a system which contemplates you as intellectual and moral beings; as beings who necessarily exert an incalculable influence, good or bad, upon each other, upon mankind, and upon the moral universe; as beings, moreover, who can never cease to exist, in a state of perfect happiness or of unutterable wretchedness. The present moment is the link which connects the *past* with the *future*;—a moment calculated to bring the past most vividly to your recollection, to awaken in your bosoms a deep and anxious solicitude respecting your future career and experience;—a moment, so full of intense interest to you and to me—so pregnant with result to every individual now before me, that I feel it difficult to determine what points of consideration I ought to select. It is your *advantage*, your individual, present and everlasting *welfare*, that I now desire to seek; and perhaps, you cannot, at this instant, be more profitably exercised, than in honestly and solemnly calling up to your recollection the days of your life that are gone.

Permit me, then, to ask you, in order that you may put the question, every one of you, secretly to himself, What views do you now entertain of your past life?

What think you of the *period of your infancy?*—when you hung a helpless, and, as it respects guilt personally contracted, a guiltless babe on your mother's breast—the tender object of a mother's care; over whom she watched day and night, with a sleepless solicitude, only known to the faithful mother? Can you think on the fond embraces of a mother's love, and the unutterable feelings awakened in a mother's bosom, when she gazed with delight on the child of her affection?—I ask, is there a man now before me, who can thus think on the days of his infancy, and compare them with the *present moment*, and his heart remain unmoved? Do you now consider how your father and mother toiled to procure, with the sweat of their brow, bread for *you* to eat, raiment for *you* to put on, a bed for *you* to sleep upon, and a house to shelter *you* from the cold, the rain, and the storm?—can you remember all this, and not put to your own hearts the question, How have I requited my parents' labour, their solicitude, their love? Oh, could they for a moment have imagined that they were rearing up children to bring dishonour upon their name, to be the inmates of prisons and of convict hulks, and to appear, covered with the badges of infamy, as you now do, on the decks of a transport, to be removed with forfeited liberty from their native land, to some distant corner of the world, there to reap the bitter fruits of folly and of crime, what would have been the agonies of your parents' hearts!

Perhaps there are before me the children of pious parents—two or three, it may be. You who are thus privileged, remember that you are the subjects of many fervent prayers. Your parents carried you, in the arms of their faith and love, to the throne of grace; and there, in the fervour of secret devotion, when no eye saw, but the Eye of Him whose help and blessing they implored for you, did they dedicate you to that compassionate Redeemer, who came to seek and save the lost!

Do you remember how they taught you the Scriptures, and led you forth on the day of holy rest to the house of God? Do you now remember the daily worship of God in your father's family, his morning and evening sacrifice of prayer and praise, his reading of God's holy word? When the hour of rest arrived, the arms of a fond mother placed you in the couch which her affection and industry had prepared; and you fell asleep, listening to the tenderest expressions of maternal love. By the bed-side of her slumbering and unconscious child she kneels in prayer. Her heart's desire and that of her husband is, above all things, to see their children become the children of God by faith in Christ Jesus, and thus make choice of that good part which shall never be taken away from them.

Do you recollect, as you advanced in years, how you set at naught all their counsel, despised their entreaties, frustrated their prayers, and, by your disobedience and ingratitude, grieved their spirit, and stung their hearts? They saw the first outbreakings of the corruptions of your nature, and laboured to see those corruptions uprooted. They observed your disposition to turn your back upon *them* and upon *God*, and they tenderly remonstrated with you on the fearful choice you were making. They saw your choice of corrupt associates, and they reminded you that he who walketh with *wise men* shall be *wise,* but that the *companion of fools* shall be *destroyed;* yet all was of no avail. Your parents fought and laboured *for you* and *for God;* you fought and contended *against yourselves, against your parents, against God!* You cared not for a father's grief or a mother's broken heart; you heeded not their counsel, you steeled your heart against their love; you were wedded to the companions of your iniquity—to your unhallowed enjoyments, and after them you were determined to go. When the messengers of peace beckoned you to return to the paths of holiness, you sullenly turned your backs, determined to take the full draught of sin, though you knew that *death* was in the cup. Thus you ran greedily in your own ways, reckless of all consequences, until justice laid her iron hand upon you, and awarded you what *by your deeds you demanded*, and the interests of society required—namely, *that you should be removed from the land of your birth, and be placed in circumstances corresponding with your character and your crimes.*

But although few of you may have enjoyed the privilege of being brought up by *consistent* Christian parents, there are, nevertheless, many advantages which all of you have possessed.

Have you not, ever since you opened your eyes upon the world you inhabit, had visible proofs of the power, wisdom, and goodness of God? Do not the heavens declare the glory of God, and the firmament show his handiwork? Do not your own bodies declare to you the perfections of Him who made you, and who has fed and upheld you all your life to the present moment? Hath he not been continually doing us good; giving us rain from heaven and fruitful seasons, filling our hearts with food and gladness, giving us life, and breath, and all things?

And what have you to say to CONSCIENCE—which God has placed in every man's bosom, by which to distinguish between right and wrong? Have you been careful to enlighten conscience? and have you listened to its voice? Do you remember, when a child, with what a clear and distinct voice conscience spake to you; told you of some immediate duty, some good act to be done, and bade you make haste and do it; or remonstrated with you as to some sinful omission, or some evil deed, warning you of consequences? And do you recollect with what conscious *sophistry* you laboured to *turn aside* her reasonings, to silence her voice, to impose upon yourself, and so to gratify your sinful desires? In this way conscience became seared as with a hot iron, and you have gathered the bitter fruits of your triumphs over her remonstrances

—you have reaped an abundant harvest of guilt, infamy, and suffering.

Have you not also received many warnings from the *dispensations* of *Divine Providence?* Have you not been visited, perhaps, again and again, with affliction?—brought, it may be, to the very gates of death; but your life was in great mercy prolonged, to give you time and space to return unto God. And how have you improved these kind chastisements? Have they produced the effect for which they were designed by a gracious God? Let conscience and your presence here answer the question.

Which of you, moreover, cannot recollect a near relative, an intimate associate, cut down by death, perhaps suddenly, or at the close of a lingering disease, during which he was, by his sufferings, preaching a loud and intelligible sermon to all around him? Was he carried off in the midst of his iniquity, while rejecting the mercy published in the Gospel? Oh, how loudly does *such a death* speak to your conscience! And could you but hear the voice, how loudly does your friend, at this moment, address you from the regions of despair and everlasting burning? Or, was he a faithful follower of Christ? How does he now beckon to you from the mansions of eternal rest, and call upon you to turn at once from paths that lead down to the abodes of death!

Has your attention never been arrested by the holy and useful lives of godly men, rich or poor—men who live above the world, humble, consistent Christians, who press forward to a blessed and glorious eternity?

Why did you not, then, follow their example, and secure to yourselves their happiness? As to your telling me that you reckoned all the avowed followers of Christ hypocrites, this is too absurd to deserve our notice. If there were no GOOD shillings, there COULD be, in circulation, no BAD ones; and if there were no *real* Christians, there would be no *hypocritical* professors of Christianity. Your conscience tells you, it was because you hated the Lord, that you hated his faithful servants; and preferred the broad way and the wide gate leading down to the chambers of death, before the narrow path and strait gate which conduct unto life.

But, again: Have you never heard of a book called the BIBLE? I ask you, most solemnly, how have you treated it? You know that it was written by men inspired by the Spirit of God, and that by the Bible, God Himself speaks to your understanding and your heart. And when God addresses us, has He not a *right* to be heard? Your Maker graciously sent to tell you of your rebellion and your danger, of His love, and the provision He has, in His great mercy, made for your deliverance, and recovery to Himself and to happiness; and what reception have you given to His message, and to His Bible, through which that message was conveyed? His message have you not refused to receive? His Bible have you not treated with indignity and neglect? You know that you have not made it your business to search it diligently, and in a right spirit; nor yielded to it the obedience which it is your duty and privilege to yield; and, *therefore,* it is, you are this day standing on these decks in your present unhappy and degrading circumstances. Obedience to your Bible would have prevented all the evil you have brought upon yourselves, and which you now of necessity must endure.

Are there many of you who tell me you cannot read, and that, *therefore*, you do not deserve blame for not reading the Bible? I ask you, why cannot you read? You knew that a written message to you from heaven must deserve to be examined; and that it must be worth your while—to say nothing of your *duty*—to use your utmost endeavours to be enabled to read and understand such a message. But what efforts, what *strenuous* exertions have you made? Had you no access, by any means, at any period of your life, to a school? How many did you beg and entreat to give you lessons? How many *refused* to afford you help? Have you not manifested a shameful *indifference* about the matter, preferring any amusement, however low or pernicious, to the manly exercise of learning to read the Scriptures? I can scarcely suppose that there is among you one individual, who might not have been able this day to read, had he done his duty, in using the means of instruction within his reach. For such wilful ignorance, and for all the crimes and sorrow that spring therefrom, is that man answerable to his conscience, to society, and to God!

Once more: You had access to *places of public worship* where the sacred Scriptures were read, prayers offered to God, and the Gospel of salvation freely published! Did you thankfully avail yourselves of every opportunity of there meeting with the people of God, to wait upon Him in His appointed ordinances?

How have you employed the first day of the week—*the Lord's day?* Look back upon your Sabbaths! What speak they now? Are you prepared to hear their voice at the judgment-seat of Christ? What do they witness? Do you tell me they witness against your *parents*, or your *masters?* These are not replies to my present questions. What testimony do your Sabbaths bear to *you?* Have you used them for the ends for which He graciously gave them to you? Did you regard the day of holy *rest* as the day of *slothful* indolence? How much of God's holy day did you spend in *idleness:* how much in sinful and gross indulgences? Where were you when you heard the tolling of the bell, when the people were gathering themselves together to hear the word of pardon and peace, of holiness and life? What said you to the *loud call,* or to the *whispers* of conscience, when your neighbours and their families were proceeding to the house of prayer? Whither did your feet carry *you?* —To the place where the blessed *Jesus* hath promised to meet, to receive, and pardon sinners, and to fill them with the joys of His great salvation? or did they bear you to the haunts of vice, the abodes of darkness and of the children of darkness—the gates of death, which lead down to hell? The *Tavern* was more suited to your dispositions, than the place of *Divine Worship;* the destructive draught from the poisoned cup was swallowed with a greedy relish, while the rich provisions of the Gospel table, and the pure water of life, were utterly loathed and rejected; dust, the serpent's meat, was preferred to the bread of heaven; low and corrupting ribaldry was more pleasing to the ear of your licentiousness, than were the truths of the Gospel. The song of the drunkard was preferred to the hymn of salvation and praise. Shame, poverty, disease, and death, were chosen rather than respectability, competency, health, and life; and you are this day reaping some of the fruits of your choice.

Finally: you knew *the laws of your country;* and that you were bound, both by the laws of God and man, to speak truth, to be honest and upright, and to wrong no man. You knew that it was your duty to be industrious and frugal; to provide, by some lawful calling, for yourselves and your families; you were perfectly aware that the peace of society required that the laws of the land should be enforced; yet these laws you deliberately, and the greater number of you, probably, oftener than once, violated. This course of conduct you moreover followed, in the face of many practical warnings, furnished to you by thousands of your countrymen, who, by their unprincipled and lawless conduct, rendered themselves obnoxious to justice, and paid the penalty. Thus have you forgotten the tender care of your parents, despised their counsels, and frustrated their prayers; the voice of faithful conscience you have stifled; the warnings of Divine Providence you have turned aside; the holy example of God's children only excited the enmity of your carnal minds; the word of God you either neglected or perverted; the house of prayer you forsook for the abodes of sin and death; on the sound of the Gospel of peace you closed your ears; the Lord's day you profaned; the laws of your country you have trampled under your feet. The judges of the land have declared, on the verdict of a jury of your own countrymen, that the peace of society demands your being placed under restraint, and forthwith removed to a distant corner of the empire; and you cannot fail to acknowledge—*provided you are now in a becoming and hopeful state of mind*—that your sentence is *just*, and that the Judge of all the earth, who knows your heart, and all your ways, hath acted towards you, not only in *righteousness*, but likewise in wisdom, and in *great mercy*.

These reflections may be painful to your minds, but they are profitable. You are, at this moment, entering upon a new career; you now come under a system of moral discipline, which contemplates, not only your present, but your future character and enjoyments through endless ages; and it is of the utmost importance that you should entertain just views of the past, and be duly prepared to enter upon what lies before you.

Should there be—the case is *possible*—one individual amongst you, who has in *truth* reason to conclude that he is not guilty of the crime imputed to him, let him remember, that however much such an evil is to be lamented, and however much *man* may have sinned in tearing him from his friends and the land of his birth, that there are *other* crimes with which he is justly chargeable before God, which deserve at his hand a far severer chastisement; and that, viewing the infliction as an evil which the All-wise and Sovereign Ruler of the universe has permitted to overtake him, it may be so improved as to advance his best interests for Time and Eternity!

I merely admit the *possibility* of such a case, knowing that it is not a rare thing for men in your situation to allege that they are *guiltless* sufferers; but the *probability* is, that there is not among you *one* individual who is not guilty of the crime or crimes with which he is charged, and on account of which he is now suffering.

You now withdraw to your berths, and you will do so in deep and solemn thought. Let every man's mind retire within himself. Let there be no talking, but let all be deep consideration. Look back upon your lives; silently meditate upon, and faithfully apply, every man to himself, what has been now spoken in great kindness to you all. Let every one consider, that to talk to his neighbour on retiring from this place, is to invade his neighbour's rights, and to interrupt that solemn and secret communion that he is now required to hold with his own heart, and with Him who is the Searcher of all hearts, and from whom no secrets are hid.

SECOND ADDRESS TO THE PRISONERS.

The following day is chiefly occupied with the organization of the people. They are formed into three divisions, and placed under the superintendence of three captains, cautiously selected from amongst their fellow-prisoners, according to the character given them in the hulks and prisons, and my own observation of their countenances and general demeanour. Besides the appointment of captains of divisions, as many more of the petty officers are nominated as can be fixed upon consistently with prudence.

In the afternoon, just in time to conclude before mustering the people below, for the night, they are assembled on the quarter-deck—the guard being on the poop—to receive the *second* address; of which the following is the substance:

SECOND ADDRESS AFTER THE EMBARKATION OF THE PRISONERS.

In my first address, I endeavoured to assist your recollections of your past lives, in order to aid you in the secret examination of your hearts, and I would hope that you have solemnly and prayerfully reflected upon what I said; and that He to whom the night is as the day, hath seen your unfeigned contrition; observed your self-abasement in His sight ; and recorded, in the book of His remembrance, the earnest longing of your souls to be delivered from sin and death, and recovered to holiness and life.

I. I now call your attention, in the *first* place, to the exercises in which you are to be occupied during the voyage; and I do not address you merely as *prisoners*, but as *my fellow-men*. Of the causes which have brought you here, I say nothing. All that I have to do with at this moment, are the facts, that *I find you here*, and that *I find myself here*, charged with the care of your persons, your health, improvement, and happiness. I look upon you as so many members of that family to which I also belong—the offspring of our common and almighty Parent, the Creator and the Preserver of the universe. He made you, and He made you *for Himself.* He made you, at the first, in His own moral image, and under His blessing; you have lost that image, and have fallen under His disapprobation. Still you are accountable to Him for all you *think;* for your *belief* and *unbelief;* for all you *say*, and for all you *do*. Not only are you accountable, but you are likewise *immortal*, beings. Every one of you is in possession of a *deathless* spirit; a spirit which must soon quit the tabernacle of clay it now inhabits, and, leaving it to return to the dust from which it was taken, must appear before God, to receive at His hand, according to the deeds done in the body, whether they be good or evil.

But He who is not a man that He should lie, nor the son of man that He should repent, hath announced to a guilty and desolate world, the joyful tidings of a Divine Deliverer. The eternal *Word*, by whom all things were made—even the beloved Son of the Father—clothed Himself in the nature of the fallen and the lost, and appeared as the "*Prince of Life;*" vanquished the great adversary, and accomplished a complete salvation for the human race. This great salvation was exhibited to the Patriarchs, and to the nation of the Jews; it was preached by the Apostles of the Lord; and in the Scriptures these glad tidings of great joy are proclaimed, at this day, to all the sinful and perishing children of men, without distinction of rank or condition; proclaimed to *you*,—for *your* deliverance from sin and its bitter fruits, for *your* recovery to God and to holy and blissful obedience. According to your treatment of this message of mercy and peace, will be your eternal condition. If you receive it, you receive pardon, life, and glory everlasting; if you reject it, you choose condemnation, death, and never-ending wretchedness. But the Holy Scriptures not only reveal to you the way of pardon and life, but all that you really require to know in the present world respecting God and yourselves; what you are to *believe*, and what you are to *practise*; the duties you owe to your Maker, to your fellow-men, and to yourselves. They inform you on what principles, and from what motives, you are to act, so as to please God. These inspired writings constitute the chart by which you are to steer your course, through the present life, to the shores of a boundless eternity! They are the magazine, wherein is laid up the whole Christian armour with which you are to meet, and to vanquish, all your spiritual enemies. They set before you the Bread of life, of which if a man eat he shall never die; the raiment, which waxeth not old; the robe of righteousness; the garments of salvation and praise. They supply you with gold tried in the fire, that you may be rich. They conduct you to that great and gracious Physician, who is able and willing, without money and without price, to heal all your wounds; to remove all your diseases; to enable your eyes to see, your ears to hear, and your hearts to receive the things belonging to your present and everlasting peace. When you are cast down, they will raise you up; when bewildered and perplexed, they will give you counsel; when in doubt as to your path, they will say to you in a language you will understand, "This is the way, walk ye in it." When your heart is disconsolate, they will fill you with that joy with which a stranger intermeddleth not; when in darkness, they will give you light; when weary and faint, they will supply you with strength, and courage, and fit you for all the demands of the day; when filled with self-loathing, they will show you in whom the Father regards you as "complete;" when elated with the joys of salvation, they will keep you humble at the foot of the cross. In health they will quicken you in the work your heavenly Father hath given you to perform; in affliction, they will enable you to exercise resignation and hope;

and holding fast the truth concerning Jesus even to the end, you will through faith in Him who died and rose again, be made more than conquerors over the last enemy, and partakers of that eternal life and glory which the Lord hath promised to all who love and obey him.

Your principal exercises during the voyage, then, will be to read the Scriptures, to search them diligently; to commit them to memory; to store your minds with their precepts and doctrines; and especially to study that grand remedial system there made known for the restoration of sinful men—and therefore of *you*—to the Divine favour, to holiness, and to bliss.

It is necessary that you should be made acquainted with some of the *evidences* of the truth and inspiration of the Holy Scriptures, that you may be able to defend yourselves from the attacks of the wicked; we shall therefore devote a portion of our time to that subject. Your attention will also be directed to the investigation of the works of creation, especially the world we inhabit, and our solar system, which is calculated to elevate our souls to God, and to fill us with wonder, admiration and praise.

But it is the Bible itself which I am most anxious that you should read and study; and you will all, I trust, be able, at the termination of the voyage, to read with so much accuracy, as to warrant my giving each of you a copy previously to your debarkation. Past experience leads me to expect to find a large proportion of you totally uneducated. If so, you will find at school abundance of employment during the voyage. Idleness can have no place with us; the whole of our time will be in demand. The most willing, cheerful, and active exertions will be required on your part, to remove the calamity under which you now lie, of not being able to read, or not with facility; and to acquire useful knowledge, especially the knowledge which God communicates to you in his word. So actively engaged will you be in the business of your education, that the period of your voyage will insensibly glide away; and you will feel that it has been too short for the delightful and profitable exercises in which you have been engaged.

When you shall have learned to read *well*, you will be allowed the additional privilege of learning to *write* and *cypher*. A number of you, moreover, will be occupied during a portion of your time, in *teaching*, and in discharging the duties of *petty officers* according to instructions which, in due time, will be issued.

II. I have, in the *second* place, to set before you the character of that *discipline* under which you are to be placed in this transport. It will be, as much as possible, a *moral discipline*, approximated in principle and end to the Divine government, or moral discipline of the universe. God is a holy God; His throne is established in *holiness;* His law is a *holy* law. In His government there is to be found nothing, properly speaking, *arbitrary*. His acts are all founded upon immutable principles of truth and justice, and dictated by infinite wisdom and love. God willeth, that is, desireth, the happiness of all His creatures; but their happiness must, in the very nature of things depend on the conformity of their character and conduct to His revealed will. *Your* happiness, then, is necessarily involved in your accomplishment of the revealed will of God.

From these considerations it is very evident, that whatever laws and regulations are enacted by man, for the government of his fellow-men, in order to be sound, safe, binding, and conducive to the happiness of the community—they must be in perfect harmony with the revealed will of the Sovereign of the universe. All human legislators are bound to bear solemnly in mind, that they are legislating for beings who are *already* the subjects of a government infinitely superior to all other governments; the subjects of a King, who has an inalienable right to their supreme affection and unlimited obedience; whose law is, in its authority, infinitely above all the enactments of the creature, and renders null and invalid every opposing or conflicting decree or command.

In laying down rules, then, for the regulation of your conduct on board this transport, it will be my care to see, that such rules are in perfect keeping with the revealed will of your Maker; so that you shall not be required to do or omit any thing which would imply an infringement of His laws; but that in obeying me, you shall be found yielding obedience to the great Ruler of us all.

It is required of you, therefore, that your language, your manners, and the whole of your conduct towards each other, be in keeping with the spirit and precepts of *Christianity.* The grand rule for your guidance is so summarily and beautifully expressed by our Lord, that when once heard it is understood; and with the slightest desire to remember it, can never be forgotten: "ALL THINGS WHATSOEVER YE WOULD THAT MEN SHOULD DO TO YOU, DO YE EVEN SO TO THEM." Keeping this rule in view, and carrying it out in the whole of your intercourse with one another, you cannot fail to secure the approbation of your own minds, and give satisfaction to me, and to all who act with me in the public service. In accordance with its spirit, it is enjoined upon you to regard each other as *brethren*, to cherish those feelings of kind and affectionate interest in each other's happiness, which become you as the offspring of one common Father, and which ought to derive a peculiar tenderness, from the circumstances in which you are placed, as *fellow-transgressors*, reaping the bitter fruit of your crimes. Although there are amongst you, unquestionably, *degrees* of guilt, yet you must remember that you are *all guilty*, and consigned to the same punishment; it is fit, therefore, that you should all sympathize with each other under such a heavy calamity. The least depraved amongst you, however, will regard the calamity of being guilty, and having *merited* punishment, as far more severe, and calling forth deeper and more tender sympathies towards each other, than the mere *endurance* of it. Compassionate and brotherly affection ought therefore to stamp the whole of your social intercourse, as companions in offence and in suffering, who are *now* giving your hearts unto God.

The opportunities, during the voyage, of exercising

the best and kindliest feelings, will be ample. United together as one large family, not only personal but relative duties must be every moment recurring., I request, therefore, that you will be continually on the watch to ascertain the duties immediately incumbent upon you; and that you will set about the performance of them with a cheerful alacrity. I entreat you to get rid at once of the debasing principle of *selfishness*. In seeking deliverance from it, you seek in the most effectual manner your own peace, and the comfort of all with whom you have to do. But if, on the contrary, you suffer yourselves to be influenced by this repulsive and degrading principle, you will not only banish peace and serenity from your own breasts, but you will excite and foment discord amongst your associates; and thus counteract all my efforts to advance their best interests. Let me, then, see every one of you habitually influenced by a spirit of self-denial and universal benevolence. Let every one *prefer his brother before himself*, seeking first of all his welfare and convenience, and then his own; or at least let his own and his brother's interest have an equal share in his regard and attention. Should you at once come under the influence of such a generous, elevating, and ennobling principle of action as this, how delightful will be the discharge of the task—if task it could then be called—which devolves upon me! Why, your government will be your own!—your own spontaneous rule; a government springing up out of the rule which each member of our large family exercises over his own heart and mind; the government of brotherly affection, and disinterested regard to the general good; the government of supreme love to God!

This being the character of our little community, our ears will never be assailed by the boisterous language, or our eyes pained by the savage tug of a grasping and all-appropriating selfishness. The calmness of our moral atmosphere will not be disturbed by the revolting contest for personal mastery, and personal enjoyment, and the appropriate language of a sordid self-seeking. We shall have no angry and selfish contests about supposed or real personal rights and privileges; but we shall hear the language of brotherly affection. Self-denial will take the place of self-indulgence, and the strife among us will be the strife of brotherly love; not who shall do least, but who shall do most for others' comfort; not who shall have this or that good thing, but who shall be most ready to waive the privilege in behalf of another.

You will not only be careful of each other's comforts, but you will be kindly watchful over each other's speech and behaviour, as well as your own. None of you will suffer evil upon his brother, but will "in anywise rebuke him;" only these rebukes will be in soft and gentle language—language suitable to one who feels himself to be more weak and erring than the brother whom he corrects, and thus his words of reproof will be like soft oil, refreshing and salutary, and which will not break the head or wound the feelings of the reproved.

You will not only be attentive to each other's comfort, language, and behaviour; but you will, with a prudent and affectionate zeal, embrace every opportunity of doing the greatest possible good to one another, and study to promote, to the utmost, your mutual happiness and highest interests.

To my instructions respecting your demeanour towards your petty officers and your schoolmasters, who will be chosen from amongst yourselves, you will be, in an especial manner, attentive. You will not only bear in mind that they act for *me*, but that the object of their appointment is *your* advantage, *your* improvement and happiness; and you will so act as to ensure to them the enjoyment of unmingled satisfaction in the discharge of their official duties.

I shall always regard any act of disobedience or impropriety of conduct towards a petty officer or schoolmaster, as more aggravated, than if such conduct were manifested immediately towards myself; and it will therefore be visited with severer expressions of my displeasure. Offences committed directly against petty officers, not merely imply that dereliction of principle which is involved in every offence, but are aggravated by more or less of meanness of spirit and baseness of disposition; they will therefore be visited with that degree of punishment which not only I, but all the sound-thinking among yourselves, must feel they deserve.

With regard to your demeanour towards the officers of the guard, and the soldiers under their command, the master of the ship, and the ship's officers and crew, let it ever be influenced by the same spirit which you have been enjoined to cultivate towards each other,

Let your language be always becoming and respectful, your manners most unequivocally polite, and your whole conduct consistent with the dictates of sound reason, and the regulations laid down for your guidance. The guard have duties imposed upon them, with which you are not, in the slightest degree, on any account whatever, to interfere. To none of the soldiers do I allow you to speak, unless in cases of necessity, and in the discharge of your duties. And when, at any time, you are addressed by any of the soldiers, you will uniformly reply in language the most becoming and creditable to you, and most suitable for them. To the sentries you are, on no occasion, to utter a word without my permission; none under the Crown are more sacred than the person and office of a sentry. Towards them you will therefore ever manifest the most watchful respect, and promptly attend to all their prohibitions. But it will be your business so to conduct yourselves, as to avoid ever coming into contact with the sentries at all, or with any of the guard, excepting in the performance of the duties required of you.

With the working of the ship or with any of the ship's duties, you are never to presume to interfere, except when your assistance may, from time to time, be required; which to avoid interference with your assigned duties, and especially your school-hours, must always be with my permission, and which you will then cheerfully and readily afford. In one word, towards all on board, you will ever cultivate the best and most kindly feelings.

At present I shall only further remind you, that I most distinctly and most positively prohibit every thing that in the slightest degree tends to corrupt the mind, destroy social harmony, and retard intellectual and moral improvement. All indecent language, low unmanly vulgarisms; all offensive slang; all profane oaths, cursing, and execration; all expressions derogatory to the honour of God, and calculated to pain the ears of those who love and reverence His name, but familiar and not displeasing to men of an opposite character; all such speech, let it be remembered, I most solemnly forbid. A regard to your best interests, present and future, a respect to good order, and a due regard to the protection which every man and boy amongst you has a right to expect from me, demand that all such language be wholly and entirely banished from amongst you.

On the same grounds, I forbid the use of all irritating and provoking speech or gestures, in your intercourse with each other; the employment of all vulgar epithets and unmanly "nicknames," the use of which always indicates a low and undisciplined mind. In a word, I most earnestly request, that you always speak to each other in plain and chaste language, such as can give no possible offence to any one, even the most virtuous and refined. If you duly recollect that you are *men*, who, though depraved, are still the highest order of beings in this world; and if you keep in mind what every man has a right to expect from another, as well as the respect which every one owes to himself, it will become easy and natural to you to employ, in all your intercourse with each other, the most becoming and respectful language. I do desire, that I may never, during our voyage, have cause to reprove any of my people for any thing unbecoming in speech or behaviour.

As nothing is more subversive of confidence and social order than falsehood and lies, it is most strictly enjoined upon you, that you do always speak TRUTH. At all hazards, whatever may be the consequence, speak nothing but what you do really believe to be true. What is more base, more wicked, than to tell a lie? What more dishonouring to the God of truth? What more injurious to society—what more deserving of punishment? With us, lying must, like other crimes, be ever visited with disapprobation; in other words, with some appropriate infliction.

Bearing *false witness*, is lying, accompanied with high aggravations; and therefore merits a severe punishment.

You are required to cultivate the strictest habits of honesty, and, according to the golden precept laid down to you, to respect your brother's property, as you would desire him to respect yours. If you are wise and virtuous enough to act on these principles, we shall not have a single case of theft during our voyage; not one case to cast a stigma upon *you*, or cause grief and disappointment to *me*. I do not, at present, remember one instance of theft, committed by my people, during any voyage, escaping detection sooner or later. But honesty arising from the fear of detection and punishment, is *not* honesty. To be honest, you must be honest *on principle:* honest, because the Sovereign of the universe commands it. Such is the honesty which I desire to see the whole of you cultivate and practise.

Again I have to request, that you unite cordially with me in endeavouring to secure the calm and profitable observance of "the Lord's day." I can have no authoritative control over your *spiritual* observance of that holy day; but it is my imperative duty so to arrange our affairs as to preserve quiet and peace, and prevent, as far as in me lies, every thing calculated to annoy or disturb those who desire to honour the Lord on His own day. The observance of the Lord's day for spiritual exercises and enjoyment, is *every man's right;* and it is my incumbent duty to preserve to every man under my care, *the uninterrupted enjoyment of that right.* To you God has given the day; and to you I am bound to secure, as far as possible, the opportunity of availing yourselves of His gift. I shall therefore take care that nothing be done on that day, save works of absolute necessity and mercy; and it will give me peculiar pleasure to see that you faithfully and voluntarily dedicate the Lord's day to the *cheerful* and *delightful* pursuit of biblical knowledge, and the *happy* observance of all Divinely-appointed ordinances, as far as circumstances permit.

Playing at cards, and every species of *gambling*, on *any* day of the week, are most positively prohibited. It is quite unnecessary for me to state here, the many strong reasons which might be urged for this prohibition. To the more reflecting and experienced among you, some of these reasons must be familiar. By all men of sound mind and good principles gambling is, in all circumstances, considered as a crying evil, and must certainly be regarded in this light by us; for it is a practice both dishonest and injurious, and totally at variance with the law of brotherly love. But even were it lawful to gamble, *we* have no time for such trifling, or for any unprofitable amusements, much less for those which are sinful. Just views of the value of time, and of the account which, "at that day," we must all render of its use and of its abuse, will not permit us to divert any portion of it from the purpose for which it is given to us. You will enjoy abundant relaxation in your night's rest, and in constant change of duty. And you will have wholesome exercise in your marches, by divisions, around the decks every evening, or as often as the weather and other circumstances will permit. Such of you as may be called to fill the situation of petty officers, will find that the zealous discharging of your duties secures to you abundance of exercise.

The youngest amongst you must now, in some measure, understand that it is in the strictest sense a *moral discipline* which I desire to see in operation on board this transport. In further proof of which I shall give orders that those irons—the badges of your disgrace—with which you are at present fettered, be removed from the whole of you, at as early a period as is consistent with the discharge of other duties; and I do most ardently hope, that when I have once caused them to be struck off, you will not, by your conduct, *demand* their being again replaced; for what can be more disgraceful to you, and painful to me, than the clanking of these irons as you walk along the decks?

GENERAL OUTLINE

OF

SCRIPTURAL INSTRUCTION.

Our main business, is with the *Bible;* its evidences, external and internal, its momentous doctrines and holy precepts, its appalling, yet righteous and even *merciful* threatenings, and its exceeding great and precious promises. Besides the course of instruction contained in the lessons appointed for the service on the Lord's day, the Scriptures are read in regular order at our daily worship; a chapter from the Old Testament in the morning, and from the New Testament in the evening, accompanied with prayer and a psalm, and by practical application to the heart and life. The catechetical mode of instruction on these and other occasions, is found in the highest degree advantageous. The men are called on in rotation, by my list, and when unable to reply, an appeal is made to the next on the list. This plan, besides securing the attention of all the people, makes the instructor acquainted with the state of their minds, and amount of their knowledge, or rather in the first instance at least, of their ignorance, and so directs him in their instruction. As there is not time to read through the whole Bible, the most important chapters are selected, in regular course, and the summary only is given of the intermediate ones, which the men are directed to read in private, and in the schools. Beginning with the books of Moses, we proceed through the most remarkable passages in the history of the Jews; the Psalms and Proverbs follow; portions of Job; the most doctrinal chapters of Isaiah, those especially which refer prophetically to the Messiah and His kingdom; a few chapters of Jeremiah, as xvii. and xxxi.; and Ezekiel, ix. xviii., xxxiii., xxxiv., xxxvi., and xxxvii.; a considerable part of Daniel; and select portions of the minor prophets. Of the New Testament, we read the whole of the Gospels by St. Matthew and St. John, portions of those by St. Luke and St. Mark, the whole of the Acts, and several of the Epistles; those to the Romans and Hebrews are particularly dwelt upon and applied.

The attention of the people is directed to the nature and perfections of God, especially to the great and fundamental doctrines of the Godhead—the personality of the Father, the Son, and the Holy Spirit, in connexion with the unity of Jehovah; to the Divinity of Jesus Christ and of the Holy Spirit; to the authenticity, genuineness, credibility, integrity, and inspiration of the sixty-six books of Holy Scripture; to the creation of the world,—man's primitive character,—his moral relation to God and to the universe,—his apostacy by disobedience,—in a word, to the inspired records of the garden of Eden. After considering the history of man's fall, we proceed to give the people a broad, impressive view of our guilt, depravity, and helplessness, as set forth in the sacred pages, as well as in those of uninspired history, and confirmed by daily observation,—especially by the experience of our own hearts; and having thus seen our absolute need of Divine deliverance, we turn to the provision of that better covenant, of which the Lord Jesus Christ, —the second Adam,—the Lord from heaven, is the ever-blessed and immutable Head. Beginning with Genesis iii. 15, and passing onwards, we observe the recorded faith, confession, and hope of the patriarchs and prophets; and consider many of the predictions concerning the MESSIAH, His Divine and human natures, united in the *one* person of Emmanuel,—His character, offices, work, and reign, and the nature and extent of His kingdom, as revealed in the Old Testament writings, particularly in the Mosaic ritual, and other types and figures. Our daily perusal of the New Testament leads us at the same time to the consideration of His incarnation and birth; His doctrines and precepts; His miracles and prophecies; and manner of teaching; His omniscience, forbearance, lowliness, and power; His holiness, compassion, zeal, and faithfulness; His obedience, sufferings, and rejection; His death, as the Divine and voluntary Substitute for sinners; His burial, resurrection, promises, and especially the great promise of the gift of the Holy Spirit; His appointment of the Apostles, His ascension in the presence of ordained WITNESSES, and entrance into the heavenly, holy place with His own blood, to appear as our great High Priest in the presence of God; the all-prevailing efficacy of His intercession, the eternity of His kingly, priestly, and prophetic offices, the coming of the Holy Spirit, the universal proclamation of the Gospel, and the conversion of sinners by the power of the truth and of the Holy Ghost; the formation and constitution of Christian Churches, and their Divinely-appointed ordinances and ministers. Man's relations and duties to God, to the churches of the saints, to his relatives, friends, neighbours, and country; to his sovereign, and all in authority, to all mankind, and to himself, come under our consideration, as well as the solemn subjects of death, judgment, and the final conflagration of this world; of hell, heaven, and eternity; and the unalterable condition of the children of God and the children of Satan after death!

But to give a view of the instructions imparted to the people in the style and manner in which they are delivered, is quite impossible. Occasional manifestations of principle and character by one or other of the prisoners, and all the incidents which occur on the voyage are made to supply useful and practical instruction.

When I ascertain, either by my own observation or otherwise, that a prisoner is under serious impressions, I privately send for him to some place of retirement, on deck, in the prison, or in the hospital; and converse with him on his state of mind, with a view of giving him suitable instruction, and discovering as much of his past history, and present feelings, as may be useful to us both. Such interviews, besides affording me an opportunity of dealing closely with individual souls, serve to direct my choice of subjects for general instruction, and my illustrations and application of Divine truth.

The people are occasionally assembled to hear an address on various other subjects of great practical importance; such as the vast value of their souls,—their immense moral influence,—the inconceivable extent to which they may yet prove a blessing or a curse to society, and be instrumental in promoting the salvation or the ruin of immortal souls;—on the extent of the intellectual and moral empire of God, the possible influence of man's example and history on all observant intelligences, and the awfully-important and responsible position in the universe, occupied by the most humble and obscure of the human race, even by the depraved and despised prisoner;—on the moral tendency on man, and on all observant and intelligent beings, of such a pardon of transgression, as should have no respect to the requirements and penalties of law;—on the intercourse and influence of holy angels and of apostate spirits, with this world's inhabitants; —on the great question, *How can God be just, while he pardons and justifies the ungodly who believe in Jesus?*—on the necessity of regeneration and sanctification, as well as of pardon and justification, for happiness and safety;—on the question, What is the Scripture doctrine concerning heaven and hell? and what do these terms import as essentially constituting heaven and hell, besides the idea of mere locality?

A somewhat extended experience of the sentiments, habits, and character of convicts, has taught me the necessity and importance of instructing them also very minutely, and very familiarly and impressively, on such points as the following, which I specify as they occur to me at the moment, without much regard to order, either as it respects their nature or importance: namely,

1. On the nature of *obedience* and *disobedience* to lawful orders and lawful authority.

2. On the evil and criminality of *lying*.

3. On using *improper speech* of any kind.

4. On *theft*. The amount of guilt not determined merely by the value of the property stolen, but by the nature of the violence offered to *law*, whether the law of God or of man.

5. On the misimprovement or theft of *time*. Robbing people of the time which belongs to them, and which is their *bonâ fide* property.

6. On *carelessness*. The true nature of the majority of those incidents commonly, but most incorrectly, called *accidents*,—the amount of *guilt* which most of them involve; and the vast importance of watchful and habitual *conscientiousness*.

7. On the crime of *drunkenness*, whether viewed in relation to God, to the drunkard, or to the community.

8. On the fact that no one can bring guilt upon any man's conscience, but that man himself.* Who brought

---

* Our esteemed author's intention here was no doubt good; but his language and illustrations are unguarded. It would be contrary to the

guilt on the conscience of *Eve?*—HERSELF. Who brought guilt on the conscience of *Adam?*—HIMSELF. Temptation is *to the tempter* an aggravated sin, but to those tempted, not a sin, but a trial; and the tempted contract no guilt, so long as they faithfully and firmly resist the temptation. It is *yielding* to temptation that involves the tempted in sin; for no one can stain my conscience with guilt but *myself*. The guilty stain can reach my conscience only through the medium of *my own will, my own consent.*

9. On the disposition often manifested by prisoners, both male and female, to charge their being "brought into trouble," as they call it, and to punishment, upon *others*. Does a Magistrate send a man to prison, or to the treadmill, because his master starved him, treated him cruelly, or would not allow him to attend, on any Lord's day, a place of Divine worship; and does he assign such reason in his "warrant" to carry the punishment into effect?—Or does he send a woman to prison, or to the cells, because "her mistress kept her sawing and splitting heavy wood, would allow her neither clothes nor shoes, but beat her on the head, broke her comb into pieces, and tore her handkerchief from her neck?" And are these the facts stated by the Magistrate in his "warrant," as furnishing the immediate ground for punishment? No! When prisoners encounter such treatment, (and of which one view only can be entertained,) they are

whole tenor of his views and of the context, to consider him as, in this passage, assailing the great doctrines of Original Guilt, and Natural Corruption. J. H. F.

tempted, it may be, to do or say something that is wrong, and not in keeping with prudent and meek submission, and so commit themselves, and supply some real or ostensible ground of punishment. They have, unhappily, forgotten 1 Peter ii., and similar portions of Holy Writ,—they have not acted with prudence.

10. On the practice of prisoners *absconding*, or absenting themselves without leave; and the attempt to justify such practice on the ground of the object which the absentee has, or professes to have, in view,—such as to visit a child or some other relative. Absconding is not only bad *morality*, but bad *policy;* the runaway can never feel secure or at peace, and is always living in the violation of law: a Christian, acting in character, cannot, of moral possibility, abscond. Should a convict be tempted to depart from the Christian character, and absent himself without leave, or should he become a Christian after he has absconded, he could not rest until he gave himself up to justice. The period of servitude to which we have voluntarily subjected ourselves, must be faithfully served; unless a remission of the whole or of a part of the sentence be lawfully obtained. The laws of God must not be violated: we must do wrong no more, but only do that which is right and well-pleasing to the Lord. What is the condition of an absconded convict on his death-bed; —of a convict dying in the very act of resisting or evading the just laws of men, and therefore, of violating the law of God? To die while persisting in the refusal to give himself up to justice in this world, is

to die in the position of the man who, with a stolen purse of gold under his pillow, refuses to restore it to its rightful owner!

11. On the notion that convicts are not cared for. GOD cares for them! Christianity cares for them! all truly godly people care for them! the angels of heaven care for them! Not only is Christianity their never-failing friend, but it inclines all who embrace it, to treat them justly, mercifully, and kindly, and with a benignant and prayerful regard for their truest comfort and happiness.

12. On the fearful tendency which prisoners but too frequently manifest, to become *reckless*, and to give themselves up to all manner of insubordination and crime. No treatment they receive can furnish any apology for such recklessness, however it may operate as an exciting *cause* of their folly and their sin.

13. On the proneness of prisoners to forget the immense value of their souls, and the *incalculable amount of good* they may be the means, in the hand of God, of conferring on each other, on their master and his household, on the community, the world, and the church; and, on the other hand, the extent of *evil* they may lend themselves to perpetrate or promote.

14. On the liability of prisoners to forget how *brief —how very brief, is the period of their existence* that is past,—how brief that entire portion of their existence which belongs to the present life! How readily do they lose sight of eternity, and of the eternal duration of their being!

15. On the fact, that no class of persons have it in

their power by conversation, consistent Christian example, believing prayer, and holy zeal, to contribute so largely, and, under the Divine blessing, so effectually, to the spiritual instruction, reformation, and happiness of prisoners, as *prisoners themselves*, continually living in the presence of each other. Prisoners are *accountable to God* for the use they make of their influence, to whomsoever that influence may extend. Let all think, with good effect, on 2 Kings v. 2—15; John iv. 28—39; and Rev. xxii. 17.

16. On the amount of suffering which vice inflicts upon the transgressor, and all his relatives and friends; and on *the vast number of relatives and other persons* affected by the conduct and condition of our convicts!

17. On the grand end which Government has in view in removing convicts to a remote colony; and the regard which prisoners are bound to pay to the attainment of that end,—thus improving their transportation for the highest purposes.

18. On the prayers which have been offered up to God for their salvation: a father's—a mother's prayers—a father's, a mother's, and it may be, a husband or wife's *broken heart!*

19. On the necessity of wholesome government and sound discipline; and the fearful effects which would certainly result from the absence of such restraint. Just punishment is an unspeakable mercy to the *State*—to the *World*—to the *Universe!*

20. On the duty of prisoners, as well as free servants, to cherish a proper *respect for their master*, and a *due regard for his interests:* to be not only

frugal of time, but punctual, methodical, and careful in the performance of their work; recollecting how much their own comfort, and that of a family, or of any establishment, depends on every servant—every member of that family or establishment—accurately moving in his own proper sphere, and punctually performing his assigned and proper quantum of duty. They are to be faithful in going messages,—not turning out of their proper path either to the right or left,—never loitering by the way, and most carefully avoiding all communication with improper and disreputable persons. In a word, they are conscientiously and watchfully to obey lawful orders, and never to speak disrespectfully of their master, or of any member of his household; they are to repudiate the character of *a tattler, a talebearer, a busy body*, and *an idler;* they are to pray for the peace and prosperity of the family or establishment to which they belong, and are to use every legitimate effort to promote both.

21. On the importance of personal and habitual *cleanliness, tidiness, moderation,* and *modesty* in their dress, which should ever be in keeping with their station in life, and in harmony with the spirit and precepts of Christianity. They are never to accept of money, or presents from any one, unless it clearly, and without all doubt, appear that such are offered on proper grounds, and with good and honourable motives.

22. On the importance of giving no more time to *sleep,* and *rest,* than duty to God and man require and allow, maintaining *as far as possible* the practice of

devoutly reading a due portion of the Word of God daily, and storing their minds with its facts and doctrines, its precepts and promises; of engaging two or three times a day in the solemn exercise of prayer, and carrying about with them the spirit of true devotion; of making every possible and lawful arrangement in order to assemble with the family for the worship of God, and to enjoy the privileges of domestic piety.

23. On the duty of co-operating with their master and fellow-servants, for the momentous purpose of securing the scriptural observance of the LORD's DAY. They are first to give themselves to CHRIST, and then to the church of Christ, and thankfully avail themselves of every lawful opportunity of meeting with His people in all those holy ordinances of His house, which were instituted by Him, and which His word requires us to observe.

24. On the vast—the unutterable importance of the uniform observation of the *Seventh* Commandment, and all the other commandments of the MOST HIGH, as set forth in the Scriptures, and especially in the New Testament. On the nature and design, the awful sanctions, the duties, obligations, and privileges of the marriage covenant; which is to be entered into lawfully, prudently, with a supreme regard to the Divine glory, and a due respect to mutual comfort, happiness, and usefulness. The bearings of that solemn covenant on the engaging parties themselves; on their temporal, spiritual, and eternal interests; and, beyond all human calculation, on the temporal and everlasting welfare

of others. The positive injunction which God hath, in His word, laid on all his believing people not to enter into marriage alliances with the people of the world—the unregenerate children of the wicked one.

25. On the necessity of convicts cultivating an humble, meek, and gentle spirit—being submissive, contented, and thankful; of ever remembering the injury they have inflicted on their country; the expense to which they have put the Government; the connexion which subsists between crime, and shame and suffering; and the reproach to which they have subjected themselves. Although persons under the influence of *vital* Christianity will think and feel correctly concerning prisoners, and will seek to do them all possible good, they must remember that mere nominal Christians, who know not the plague of their own hearts, and have not felt the power of the love of Christ, cannot be expected to have the same Christian sentiments towards them; so that they must lay their account to meet with much reproach, scorn, and contempt from the people of the world; and must learn meekly to submit to it,—never answering again, but secretly, in faith and prayer, committing themselves to Him who judgeth righteously, and who, even in their low and degraded estate, will never leave—never forsake them. They are now to seek, according to the Divine will, that the evil which they have brought upon themselves be overruled, and, in great mercy, made subservient to the advancement of God's glory, and their own and each other's good. They are to keep always in their hearts those gracious words, "Cast thy burden upon

the LORD, and He shall sustain thee;"* "In all thy ways acknowledge Him, and He shall direct thy paths;"† "When a man's ways please the LORD, He maketh even his enemies to be at peace with him;"‡ "Cease from anger, and forsake wrath; fret not thyself in any wise to do evil."§ They should study closely the whole of Psalm xxxvii.; and while they make a proper use of Psalm lxxxix., especially of verses 30—34, they must be constantly familiar with that most valuable and suitable chapter, 1 Pet. ii., and ever abide under the sanctifying and conforming influence of the example of Christ, and of all the precepts and promises of His Gospel.

But the points on which the prisoners are most frequently and prayerfully urged, are their individual guilt and danger as sinners in the sight of God; the perfection, suitableness, and freeness of the salvation of Christ; the scriptural facts, that it is commanded to be proclaimed to every member of the human family, and that every individnal who hears it, is by the Lord himself *commanded* to believe it, and obtain pardon and purity, life and joy. The momentous but neglected doctrine, that all men, as subjects of the Divine government, are under a moral obligation to give an *immediate* and unhesitating credit to the testimony of the Most High, to whatever subject it may relate, and are therefore bound to believe his testimony concerning the Lord Jesus Christ, as the all-sufficient and only Saviour of sinners,—is continually kept before

---

* Psa. lv. 22. ‡ Prov. xvi. 7.
† Prov iii. 6. § Psa. xxxvii. 8.

the minds of the people, and pressed upon their understanding and conscience. To refuse to believe the testimony of God is to adopt with reverence the language of an inspired apostle, "to make Him," or pronounce Him to be, "a liar!" and, therefore fearfully to increase our guilt and danger. Jesus, the Son of God, is revealed in the Scriptures, as the Substitute for sinners, who by His obedience and death hath brought in everlasting righteousness; and sinners of every class and condition are authorized and required in the Scriptures to avail themselves of it, and by faith to put on that glorious righteousness for justification, and acceptance, for present and everlasting peace. This robe of righteousness, this wedding garment, this linen clean and white, is exhibited in the inspired Scriptures to these "prisoners of hope," and they either by faith throw off the filthy rags of their own righteousness, and put it on; or they hold fast their own unseemly rags, and choose to continue and to perish in the attire of their iniquity, rather than be saved in the Divinely-provided raiment of the believing children of God.

Those who have been enlightened by Divine truth, must be deeply and firmly convinced, that nothing is capable of producing a *radical* and *permanent* improvement in the character and habits of man, but just views of *himself* and of his MAKER; and that such views are to be obtained only from that revelation which the Father of mercies has been graciously pleased to give us. Even the most *amiable* and *moral* among us are, in the sight of God, dead in trespasses and sins, until, through belief of the Gospel, they become a new creation in Christ Jesus, by the quickening influences of the Spirit of truth and holiness; and the same Almighty power is necessary for the conversion to God of a *convict*.

And not only must both the moral and the vicious experience that saving change before they can do any thing upon *right principles ; but, even keeping their eternal salvation out of view*, little good is, in my apprehension, to be expected from what is commonly called "the *crime class* of our population," until brought under the illuminating and sanctifying power of the Scriptures, and the gracious influences of the Holy Spirit; for they will, with few exceptions, persevere in a course of iniquity, the bane of social order, and totally unworthy of confidence, until they are brought back to God and to godliness, by the faith of the Gospel. Change of heart is the only ground on which I expect satisfactory change of conduct. So accustomed are some of them to vice ; so hardened in iniquity ; so utterly devoid of all sense of propriety and decorum; so insensible to the excellencies and attractions of virtue; so sunk in their own estimation, and (*as they apprehend*) in the estimation of mankind; that, if we desire to see these unhappy men become worthy of that degree of trust, without which they cannot be safely permitted to mingle in general society, *we shall aim at nothing short of their conversion to God.* It is my sober conviction, that nothing less than a saving change of heart will warrant our placing confidence in the more hardened and depraved of those who suffer transportation, or furnish a sufficient guarantee that they will prove safe and useful members of the community. The same observations will, I believe, equally apply to thousands of our population, who escape the punishments both of imprisonment and transportation.

Supreme love to God is not only the principle upon which alone we can perform even a single work acceptable in His sight, but it also secures active and unwearied obedience to the *whole* of His revealed will. Supreme love to God admits of no substitute. But let this holy and heavenly principle be, by the Spirit of God, generated in any man's heart, and, from that moment, he is under the influence of a mighty and transforming power;—a power, the tendency of which is, to diffuse itself throughout his whole nature, and reduce to its own holy character all that he is and feels, thinks and does.

Entertaining these sentiments,—held in common, I believe, by all true Christians,—it is incumbent upon us to use every possible means, in dependence on the Spirit of all grace, to bring the minds and hearts of the prisoners into contact with the momentous truths of the Gospel. He alone, who created the soul at the first, can create it *anew* in Christ Jesus unto good works. The same Almighty power which called into existence an archangel, is requisite to turn the apostate heart of man back again to God, and to restamp upon it the Divine image. Salvation is wholly of the Lord.

In dealing with convicts, it is necessary that our minds be constantly under the influence of these views.

We cannot too completely set aside *self* as nothing—less than nothing—sinful dust and ashes; nor too deeply feel that it is utterly impossible for us to impart to the mind of a fellow-sinner a single truly spiritual idea. We must consent to become as the rough unpolished horn of the priests before the walls of Jericho, and, as it were, to be merely spoken through, to our fellow-sinners, by the Spirit of all truth and grace. And we cannot put too much confidence in God, that He will give efficacy to His own word; nor too earnestly plead with Him, in humble and scriptural prayer, on behalf of those whom at His command we seek to bring to Himself. Proceeding thus, we are warranted to expect that the God of all mercy will, through our humble instrumentality, speak to the heart of the convict, and, by the moral renovation of his nature and principles, ensure the conformity of his life to the spirit and precepts of the Gospel, as well as to the laws of the land: "Not unto us, O Lord, not unto us, but unto Thy name give glory, for Thy mercy and for Thy truth's sake." (Psalm cxv.)

LAST ADDRESS.

After tracing the gracious providence of God in any circumstances of the voyage which may afford occasion for special thanksgiving, I proceed nearly as follows:

OUR eventful voyage has come to a close, and our interesting sojourn together on board this transport terminates with to-morrow's dawn. The time which has been thus occupied, forms a most important period of your existence. The providence of God has been conspicuously and graciously exercised towards you. You have been collected from all quarters of the British empire,—some of you from foreign nations,— and placed, for four or five months under a course of instruction, the grand object of which is to restore you to the knowledge, favour, and likeness of God, and to fit you for serving and enjoying Him for ever!

There is not among you, to the best of my knowledge, a man or a boy who has not declared, in the Divine presence, that he believes himself to be a guilty, lost sinner, and JESUS to be the only Saviour from sin and from the wrath to come. The question now is, What has been secretly transacted between your own hearts and God? Have you *felt* the enormity of your guilt? Have you been made *deeply sensible* of the depravity of your nature? Have you been humbled to the very dust under a just apprehension of your crimes, committed against your country's laws, against society, and against God? And have you, in very deed, come, in deep contrition of heart, to "the Fountain opened for sin and for uncleanness"—even the fountain of the blessed Redeemer's atoning blood—and, by washing in that fountain, have you had your sin all taken away, and obtained deliverance from its *wages* and its *power?*

Think now on all the truth which has been declared to you; think on the tenderness of your heavenly Father's love, the unsearchable riches of Christ's redeeming grace, the faithful and gracious strivings and long-suffering of the Holy Spirit; think on the blessedness you secure to yourselves by receiving the salvation published to you in the Gospel, and the ceaseless wretchedness which by your *rejection* of the Saviour, you deliberately choose.

I have endeavoured, though in much weakness, to declare unto you the whole counsel of God; and have kept back from you no truth He hath revealed for your instruction and salvation, and which time and ability have permitted me to declare, invariably entreating you to bring all I have said to the test of His word—thereby to prove all things; rejecting whatever is at variance with its spirit and precepts, and holding fast only that which is in accordance with the Divine mind. I humbly trust that I am free from the blood of all of you as it respects your instruction. *With Jesus Christ set before you in the Scriptures, and the command of God that you should believe in Him for salvation, addressed to you—if you perish, you perish!* But know that you perish *in the wilful rejection of God's deliverance!*

Let us remember, that a fearful responsibility attaches to us all. I am responsible for my fidelity in teaching you the way of life; and you are responsible for the use you make of all the truth that has been set before you, because it is written, (Luke viii. 18,) "Unto whomsoever much is given, of him shall much be required;"—"Take heed, then, how ye hear," (Matt. xi. 24,) Oh, take heed how you treat the Son of God! Not one of you can go on shore as you came on board! You all disembark to-morrow morning, either improved in character, or fearfully hardened. All of you have had the salvation of Christ fully and freely pressed upon your acceptance; and every one of you leaves this vessel in the character of one who has either *accepted* or *rejected* it! Oh, let me beseech you to lay this to heart, and to remember, that you carry along with you that Bible, according to which you shall be *judged at the last day!*

You, who have professed to embrace Christ as all your salvation and all your desire, I most earnestly beseech to be very watchful over your future conduct. Recollect that you are not your own, but bought with a price, and are under the highest obligations to serve Him who purchased you to Himself by His precious blood. Remember what is required of him whom the Scriptures denominate a temple of the Holy Ghost. Keep steadily in mind the tendency of your example; and recollect that your individual example must be productive of incalculable good or evil. The eyes of men and of angels are upon you; God Himself is the constant witness of your thoughts, temper, and conduct; and *the believer's God is a consuming fire*, and cannot spare, in the objects of His new covenant love, the dross of corruption and sin. Oh! remember that He requires all His children to be holy, even as He is holy—holy in heart, holy in speech, holy in conduct. Remember that the tendency of holy living, is, to *win souls* to Christ and to a participation in the blessings of everlasting life; and that the tendency of unholy living, is, to destroy souls, and consign them to the regions of eternal fire. Forget not that you have no evidence of the reality of your faith in Christ, if it sanctify not your heart and life.—If the tree is good, the fruit *must* be good; if the fruit is bad, the tree *must* be also bad. If you are living branches of the true Vine, you will exhibit, not merely the green leaves of a scriptural profession, but such fruit of holy living, as will redound to the glory of your Father who is in heaven.

Beware of the first approaches of temptation to sin, whether in thought, desire, word, or deed. Oh! be on your guard against *new* temptations; and let me earnestly beseech you, ever to bear in mind, that your only safety lies in *habitually abiding in Christ, and relying on His strength*. Be assured, that severed from Christ you have no security! If He does not hold you up, and keep you clinging to Him in faith, love, and holy obedience, you will most assuredly fall, bring fresh guilt upon your conscience, grieve the Holy Spirit, destroy your peace, give the enemies of God occasion to blaspheme, endanger your future usefulness, and perhaps inflict such spiritual injury upon yourselves, that you may perform the remainder of your journey halting, even to the borders of your grave! Take heed, then, watch and pray, that ye enter not into temptation. Keep your hearts with all diligence, and, with the heart, keep the door of your lips. At the very first approaches of sin, flee away —flee to the Cross, escape to your knees, wrestle in prayer for the needed deliverance, and *cease not*, until, through Divine grace, you *have obtained the victory;* for be ye well assured, that if you do not destroy your spiritual enemies, they will destroy you! It is not enough that you offer up cold, heartless petitions, and then return to the influence of the temptation, you must *agonize* in prayer, you must keep aloof from the temptation, in thought, in look, and in approach; it must be driven far hence from your soul, or your soul must flee far hence from the temptation. You must *abide* in Christ; and *walk* in the Spirit; you must think on your heavenly Father's love; have your conversation in heaven; and not lift off your eyes from Jesus, but contemplate Him in His sufferings, and in His glory; looking forward to the period, when you shall see Him as He is, and when He shall present to His Father, without spot and blameless, all who while on earth cultivated holiness, and followed Him in the regeneration of their hearts.

Recollect the duties which Jesus Christ hath been graciously pleased to enjoin on all his followers: your duties to God and to man. With considerable minuteness they have been set before you during your voyage. You will find them all in the pages of your Bible, which you are required diligently and prayerfully to search. In all things follow out your Bible, and you will be a blessing to all with whom you may come in contact, and therefore to the whole colony. Be faithful to *God*, according to the requirements and spirit of His word; and you will be faithful also to *man*.

I particularly urge upon you the necessity of cultivating great tenderness of conscience, and extreme *exactness* in the discharge of duty. Be conscientiously attentive to every minute circumstance connected with your duty. Guard against inattention to what may be considered *little things,* which go to make up a great deal of the sum of human life, and a due regard to which will contribute, in no small degree, to stamp your character, and affect the comfort of all with whom you have to do. The great fault of that valuable portion of the community called "servants," generally, is, the neglect of the *minor points,* of their duty—negligence as to "little things." The consistent Christian will, in *every thing,* scrupulously guard against *every* just cause of offence. He will be thoughtful, attentive, considerate; accustom himself to reflect, and remember every injunction laid upon him; and will perform every duty heartily, and to the best of his ability, to the Lord, and not merely to man.

Let me beseech you to walk humbly, closely, and habitually with God. Manifest the spirit of your Lord and Master, doing good to them that hate you, praying for them that despitefully use you, and cherishing love and good-will even to your bitterest enemies. It is through much tribulation that you are to enter into the kingdom of heaven; but to Him who died for you, and is now exalted at the right hand of the Majesty on high, be ye faithful; and although you may be called, while in this world, to pass as it were through fire and water, He will, according to His promise, bring you at last into a wealthy place.

To you who have, up to the present moment, put the gift of God, Christ Jesus, away from you, and have refused to accept of pardon and of life, I can say only a few words. Remember that the free and unfettered salvation of the Gospel has been fully declared to you. You have *now* "no cloak for your sin." You have heard the voice of the Holy Spirit speaking to you in the words of His servant John, "*Behold the Lamb of God who taketh away the sins of the world!*" You have heard His words by the Apostle of the Gentiles, "Believe in the Lord Jesus Christ, and thou shalt be saved;"* and again, by John, "He that believeth on the Son of God hath everlasting life: and he that believeth not the Son of God shall not see life, but the wrath of God abideth on him."† Oh! be persuaded to accept of Him, who of God is made unto us wisdom, and righteousness, and sanctification, and redemption. Can it be that there stands before me a man or a boy who has formed the ungrateful and desperate resolution, *that his last act on board this transport shall be a repetition of his* REJECTION OF CHRIST; and that in setting his foot on these shores, he will do so in the character of an enemy of God, a contemner of His mercy, a despiser of His covenant, and a slave of sin, who refuses to be a partaker of the glorious liberty of the children of God?

Let me entreat you to improve the moments you are yet permitted to spend on board. Let this night record your submission to God by the belief of His testimony concerning His Son Christ Jesus. Let

* Acts xvi. 31. † John iii. 36.

there be this night joy among the angels in heaven over the return of every wandering prodigal among us. Remember, that, wherever you are in this world, whatever you may be engaged in, it is still *true* that JESUS is the Saviour of sinners; and that him who cometh to Him, He will in no wise cast out. But oh! recollect, it is also true, that every hour you live in sin, and in the neglect of the mercy of God published in the Gospel, you render your heart harder and harder, fearfully increase the sum of your guilt, and make your conversion to God, *morally*, more and more improbable. If you listen to the dictates of heavenly wisdom, you will *now* credit what God saith unto you in His Word: you will at once flee for refuge to Jesus, and yield yourselves wholly up to the Lord, to be qualified by His Spirit for serving and enjoying him for ever! Then, indeed, will your stay upon the earth, whether of short or long duration, be marked by the blessed effects of Divine love upon your hearts; your light will shine before men, and commend to all around you the glorious gospel of the blessed God. But if you persist in refusing to submit yourselves unto God in the faith and obedience of the Gospel, you not only consign your souls to eternal destruction, but give no reason to calculate on your ever proving trustworthy members of society. I tell you candidly, I myself could place no unhesitating confidence in any of you as members of my family, unless your temper and conduct gave scriptural evidence of your *conversion to* GOD. And I am quite prepared to hear, that such of you as have no fear of God, nor conscientious regard for his approbation, will not be many days in the colony before you yield to temptation, fall into some crime, bring more infamy upon your character, and subject yourselves to additional sufferings. All I can now do for you is, to warn you, beseech you, and pray for you.

I solemnly repeat my warning respecting *disobedience* to any lawful command of those in authority over you. Remember that DISOBEDIENCE *to lawful commands is one of the greatest and most pernicious crimes of which you can be guilty.* What expelled angels from heaven, and converted them into *devils?* —DISOBEDIENCE. What separated our first parents from God, and subjected them and their offspring to the loss of holiness and happiness?—DISOBEDIENCE. What is the cause of all the misery and death that abound in the world?—DISOBEDIENCE. What is the cause of your present and future sufferings?—DISOBEDIENCE. What was it that prepared hell?—DISOBEDIENCE. And what did man's *disobedience* require ere man could be restored to purity and to bliss?—Nothing less than the incarnation, sufferings and OBEDIENCE, even unto death, of the Son of God! Can any of you, then, think lightly of disobedience? Let the *occasion* of your disobedience be what it may; let the thing about which you are disobedient be as insignificant as the turning of a straw; if the command be *lawful*, and you disobey that command, you are guilty of the HEINOUS TRANSGRESSION OF DISOBEDIENCE— you are chargeable with *that sin* which expelled the angels from heaven, and which lost a world! Study 1 Sam. xv. 22, 23.

I would also entreat you to remember what has been said to you respecting improper and dangerous associates. Avoid, as much as possible, the company of wicked men, the tendency of whose example must ever be to *destroy* you. Let them feel the benign influence of good example and of good counsel, but remain not in their society when it can be avoided. When it cannot, then recollect that you owe it to God, to them, and to yourselves, to be *faithful*. Be faithful to your Bible, and you will not only be kept from falling yourselves, but your conduct will call the attention of your associates to Him, who can effectually save both you and them from sin and death.

The greatest snare to which you will be exposed on shore is the use of *intoxicating liquors;* no vice is more calculated to lead you into the practice of other vices than drunkenness; it proves the overthrow of more prisoners than any other evil habit whatever. Take heed, then, that you never permit one drop of the intoxicating and destructive poison to cross your lips, unless prescribed by a medical practitioner for disease—a circumstance which is not likely often to happen.

With reference farther to your future conduct, let me hope that you will all benefit by past experience. You have already had sufficient proof of the connexion between *evil-doing* and *suffering;* you have now found out that "the way of transgressors is hard;"*

* Prov. xiii. 15.

and that the tendency of their "perverseness" is to "destroy them:"* I trust you will now experience, that wisdom's "ways are ways of pleasantness, and all her paths are peace."† Most, if not all of you, are now able to compare the peace and comfort connected with well-doing, with the infamy and wretchedness which spring from evil-doing; and I beseech you to profit by the experience. Some of you have long felt the pain and remorse that are the fruits of ignorance, irregularity and crime; why then should you desire to drink deeper in the cup from which you have already taken so many bitter draughts? Remember the gracious remonstrance of the God of Israel with his ungrateful and rebellious children: "Hear, O heavens; and give ear, O earth; for the Lord hath spoken: I have nourished and brought up children, and they have rebelled against Me. . . . . They have forsaken the Lord, they have provoked the Holy One of Israel unto anger, they are gone away backward? Why should ye be stricken any more? ye will revolt more and more: the whole head is sick, and the whole heart faint. From the sole of the foot even unto the head, there is no soundness in it; but wounds, and bruises, and putrefying sores: they have not been closed, neither bound up, neither mollified with ointment."‡ The people for whom God had done so much, remained insensible to His goodness and mercy, turned their backs upon Him, and subjected themselves to severe and repeated expressions of the Divine dis-

* Prov. xi. 3. † Prov. iii. 17. ‡ Isa. i. 2, 4—6.

pleasure. And did their character improve under the chastening hand of God? Did they seek, in deep humility and contrition, the sanctified use of their multiplied afflictions? No; they persevered in the obstinacy of their rebellion, and called for more strokes from the rod of their Almighty and long-suffering Father, until they were smitten all over, and covered from head to foot with wounds, and bruises, and putrefying sores.

And have not *you* long abused the loving-kindness and sparing mercy of the Lord? Have not *you* lamentably misimproved the repeated chastisements to which your repeated offences have subjected you, and grievously provoked the Divine displeasure? Why should you subject yourselves to be stricken any more? Why should you be *imprisoned* any more? Why should you be *ironed* any more? Why should your flesh be lacerated by the *scourge* any more? Why should you subject yourselves to any more of the penalties of the law? Have you not already tasted enough of the bitterness of transgression? Have you utterly cast off all desire for the approbation of God? Have you calculated the consequences of perseverance in rebellion against Him? Oh! have you thought of the agonies which you are laying up in store for yourselves, by your *voluntary rejection* of the Son of God? Are your hearts not affected by the consideration of the pernicious influence of your example? A world that has broken loose from its proper orbit may carry far and wide physical ruin and confusion among surrounding worlds; but the irregular course of one sinner, of one convict, may be productive of far greater evil,—his path may be marked by a more fearful devastation: his lawless progress away from the Sun of Righteousness, must be seen in the terribleness of its moral havoc among the immortal souls of men; perhaps among beings also of a higher order; and his character and destiny are those of the "wandering stars, to whom is reserved the blackness of darkness for ever!"*

Hear, then, all ye whose hearts, up to the present moment, have been stout against the Lord: hear ye again the proclamation of mercy, "As I live, saith the Lord God, I have no pleasure in the death of the wicked; but that the wicked turn from his way and live: turn ye, turn ye from your evil ways; for why will ye die, O house of Israel?"† "Be ye reconciled unto God. For He hath made Him who knew no sin to be sin for us, that we might be made the righteousness of God in Him."‡—"He that heareth My word, and believeth on Him that sent Me, hath everlasting life, and shall not come into condemnation; but is passed from death unto life."§ Suffer me to implore the whole of you, not to add another hour to the period of your rebellion and unbelief. Look unto JESUS, and live! Cleave to Him with purpose of heart; follow Him fully; holding fast the beginning of the confidence, and the rejoicing of the hope FIRM UNTO THE END.‖

To-morrow morning you quit this vessel; a vessel

---

* Jude 13.
† Ezek. xxxiii. 11.   ‡ 2 Cor. v. 20, 21.
§ John v. 24.   ‖ Heb. iii. 6, 14.

the remembrance of which must be for ever associated with your future destinies, be they what they may; whether the destinies of the despisers of mercy, or of the humble followers of the Lamb of God. Of our conduct on board this ship, of our treatment of Christ, and of His great salvation, you and I must render an account!

We shall all meet again—I say that *we shall all meet again!* It may not be in this life. But we shall meet with an assembled world, together with *holy* and with *fallen* angels. *We* shall form part of that awful assembly which will be present on the Day of Judgment, and in the proceedings of that day we shall not be mere spectators; no! but we shall be personally and intensely interested. Let us now choose the position we shall occupy in the presence of the JUDGE. Let us now decide whether we shall look up with joy, and behold in Him our blessed Advocate and High Priest, engaged in His new-covenant love to save us, and to bring us to glory; or whether, under the overwhelming power of conscious guilt, we shall cry to the rocks to fall on us, and hide us from the wrath of the LAMB, and from the glory of His power. Oh! let every one of us now choose, whether our abode shall be with the unbelievers and the unholy, in *everlasting burnings*,* or with the sanctified in Christ Jesus, whose names are written in Heaven, and whom the blessed Saviour will present faultless before the presence of His glory, with exceeding joy.†

* Isa. xxxiii. 14. † Jude 24; Matt. xxv.; Isa. xxxv.

May God, in His abundant and great mercy, grant that all the prisoners whom He hath been pleased, on repeated occasions, to commit to my care, during the passage to Australia, and all those whom I have addressed in the Colony, may be graciously led "into all truth;" and, under the abiding influence of the Saviour's love shed abroad in the heart by the Holy Spirit, be preserved in the faith and obedience of the Gospel to everlasting life, unto the praise of the glory of the riches of Divine grace. And may all *other* prisoners be duly instructed in the knowledge of the sacred Scriptures, and as "prisoners of hope"* flee for refuge† to the atoning blood of the Cross, giving evidence that they have surrendered their hearts to the Lord, by walking in His footsteps, under the sanctifying influences of His Spirit, and in accordance with His blessed will, as set forth in His written and inspired Word.

COLONIAL TESTIMONIES

CONCERNING CONVICTS BY THE "EARL GREY," AND FORMER SHIPS.

Inquiries have frequently been made in England respecting the behaviour, after their arrival in the colony, of prisoners who made a profession of faith in Christ while under my charge. But it is not possible for me to give a satisfactory reply to such inquiries, because circumstances do not admit of my obtaining

* Zech. ix. 12. † Isa. lx. 8; Heb. vi. 18.

adequate information. which ought to be not only correct, but minute and circumstantial. My stay at Hobart Town has always been so short as to give me little opportunity of tracing their history; for they are scattered about at different, and sometimes distant stations, and when they obtain their freedom they sometimes withdraw from Van Diemen's Land, and settle in some of the other Australian colonies.

I am thankful to be able to state, however, that *all I have learnt* concerning those men who gave evidence of reformation on board, has in general been *most satisfactory.*

One gentleman sent me a message, to the effect, that if I had brought out any more *such men* as those he obtained from one of my former ships, he wished to have two of them, *for he never had such servants on his farm before.*

Another gentleman, who engaged a man from my earliest ship, has for *many* years entrusted him with the superintendence of some works, at a large salary; and he assured me, that he believes there is not a better man in the country. Several of my men have been placed also in confidential situations, under Government officers.

A minister of Christ lately testified to me, on his own knowledge, that one of my men by the *Elphinstone,* a shepherd by occupation, had walked most consistently according to the spirit and precepts of the Gospel, for a period of three years and a half prior to the date of his communication; and, that in the district in which his lot was cast, he was known amongst the people as "*the good shepherd,*" so singularly excellent was his Christian character.

Through private channels I have received most gratifying information respecting other individuals who had been under my care; but that information is not so extensive as I should desire, nor is it communicated in such a shape as to warrant my giving it to the public. Having no memoranda at present within my reach, many men, of whom I had a good report, have escaped my memory; but I can count up between forty and fifty whom I know to have been conducting themselves with great propriety, and to be doing well in various situations, under private masters—in government employ—or, in trades and business on their own account.

Of the men who arrived by the *Earl Grey*, I received when last at Hobart Town, after they had been two years and a half in the colony, the most pleasing reports. Several of them, including two who were most active and useful during the voyage, I saw, and was delighted with their apparent steadfastness in the faith and obedience of the Gospel; moreover several of those men who did not appear, while on board, to have been deeply impressed by Divine truth, were credibly reported to me as having turned to the Lord since they landed, or rather since they had been emancipated from the baneful influence of the Probation Gang. A letter is subjoined, from one of the men who had been most active and useful to me in the *Earl Grey*, written after he had finished his term of probation, which, along with other evidence which I have received, proves the satisfactory tone of his mind, and that he had so far stood the test of close contact with unreformed convicts of the most wretched and debased character.

It was the intention of the late Comptroller-General, Captain Forster, to supply me with a list of my men, exhibiting their colonial character as it stood in his books; but that officer was removed by death before his intention was accomplished; and those who understand the nature of such official reports, know that they can but imperfectly assist us in forming a just estimate of the moral principles and character of the men to whom they refer. I must, therefore, content myself with giving a few extracts from various authentic documents, and would only observe that in giving these extracts respecting the prisoners, I am placed under the painful necessity of including portions which allude to myself; but I hope they will be viewed as referring to *the system of instruction and discipline* which I endeavour to carry into effect, rather than as alluding *to me personally.*

EXTRACTS FROM A LETTER OF A CONVICT

WHO WENT OUT BY THE "EARL GREY;"

DESCRIBING "PROBATION."

The following letter was written by W. B., a convict often referred to as one of my most efficient helpers on board the "Earl Grey," and contains the history of some of my men after they landed. It is fitted to excite a spirit of prayer for unhappy convicts, and to open the eyes of some in our land, who are so deluded as to count transportation a boon!

... "Surely it becomes me to unite with the church as she sings, Isa. xii., 'O Lord, I will praise thee; though thou wast angry with me, thine anger is turned away, and thou comfortest me. Behold, God is my salvation; I will trust and not be afraid, for the Lord Jehovah is my strength and my song; he also is become my salvation.' Oh, it is heaven in the soul of the poor sinner, deserving only present and eternal misery, when he can say and feel, without presumption and without hesitation, 'God is *my* salvation!'

"A new scene in life has just begun with me. For two years and upwards I have been serving under 'Probation,' and a *trying time* I found it; but, thank the Lord, I can now breathe a purer air, and can lift up my head (*as far as a convict can*) once more in society, having just escaped from the dreadful society of the Probation Gang. . . . I need not attempt to describe the anxious solicitude I have felt about you and my child. My heart has often ached when I have thought of you. Most of my letters, (which I doubt whether you ever received,) were written 'in the Bush,' with a flat stone for my table, and a sheet of bark, from the peppermint-tree, for my seat—a spot rendered dear to me, as the place of retreat where I often found the Lord's saving and consoling presence.

"My object in now giving you a history of my past sufferings, is to give you a true description of the poor prisoner when banished in consequence of crime, and to awaken your tenderest sympathies and most earnest prayers for your suffering brethren and sisters here; 'tis not to utter a *complaining* word, for I feel I deserve tenfold more punishment, or rather chastisement, than any which I have as yet received. Thanks to the Lord, I am not in hopeless misery in hell!

"On Jan. 14, 1843, we arrived here; and in a few days were separated, and most of us sent into the interior, to our appointed stations. Previous to our dispersion, we had an opportunity of assembling for reading the Scriptures and prayer, as we had been wont to do on board the ship. We all lodged in one poor sorry outhouse, near the barracks, the first night we spent on shore in Van Diemen's land. My dear companions were all asked if they would unite once more together, most likely for the last time,—a proposal to which they all agreed without one dissentient voice; and earnest were the prayers, and deep the feeling, on behalf of our kind friend and patron we were about to part with; and fervently, too, we sought Divine wisdom and grace, to guide and bless us in all our future steps.

"The time soon came for us to be marched off. Myself and five more shipmates, with twenty old hands, were yoked to carts loaded with picks and other heavy goods. An overseer took command, and at the well-known sound, 'Go on!' off we started, not knowing where; all we knew was that we were going to form a new station, fifty miles up the country. We had not proceeded many miles before I began to feel exhausted; for just stepping on shore, after a long voyage, you may suppose I was unfit for hard travelling; added to this, my health was but delicate; but journey on we *must*, up rugged hills, beneath a scorching sun, and amid the hellish oaths and imprecations of our new companions. My ears were unaccustomed to such wicked words as proceeded from their lips. One particular oath, the first time I heard it uttered, made me shudder, and that was from a poor gray-headed man when oppressed with dragging those heavy carts. It is too awful and too grossly blasphemous to admit of being written; its purport was a wish that he might die that moment, if he moved another step; but the Lord had mercy on him, and did not grant his request, for he still moved on. I earnestly asked the Lord to stay the poor thing in his progress to perdition. Surely, I thought, I shall never hear such language again; but in this I was greatly mistaken, for it is common, awfully common, to hear prisoners, and officers too, swear the same oath. The Lord have mercy on this devoted colony!

"We arrived at ——, and were put within the prison; and a sad night I spent as to outward circumstances. We were nearly covered with ——, and other filth, so that we could not lie down. My friend and shipmate who was with me on board the hulk, desirous of doing good, proposed to read a chapter from 'God's word;' but oh! I shall never forget the dreadful cry they set up! 'You old hypocrite! There's no God in Van Diemen's Land, nor shall there be!' were the blasphemous words vociferated. Poor things! *they* had no kind and pious surgeon-superintendent to bring them out, to instruct and reform their minds, as we had. How thankful should we be, and how great our responsibility! Not till then did I find banishment such a *heavy* chastisement. To be obliged to hear and see what has passed before me, the past two years, is a severe and heart-rending affliction.

"Morning came, and we pursued our journey. We had to traverse the Bush, with scarcely a track to guide us. Here and there we saw a tent, or met a settler. The country became more rugged, but we were compelled to drag and labour on, a very hot day, until we were nearly exhausted. Night came on; and truly thankful I was to lie down upon the ground, to obtain a little repose. We encamped in the Bush, with no other shelter but God's own beautiful sky, bespangled with stars. Here we found water,—a great blessing to us, for we were parched with thirst, from the want of water during the day. Next day, on we went. The Lord was very merciful to me, for I began to feel myself more fit for the remainder of the journey, and early in the evening we arrived at the spot to which we were ordered. I have been particular in describing this journey, for the circumstances connected with it made a powerful impression on my mind. Never did I see beings sunk so low. Here I beheld the fearful effects of the fall. It led me to look at my own character and condition, as set forth in the Bible. The blasphemous expressions respecting the Holy Comforter produced horror in my mind for the moment; but I hope they also led me more earnestly to implore His gracious presence and power in my soul.

"At —— we commenced our work. . . . Then began the course of government and discipline to which I have been subjected. Gangs marched to the station as it enlarged, from ——, and ——, and other Second Sentence stations. These men are supposed to have been reformed; but, alas! their conduct soon evinced that the treatment they had received was calculated to harden, rather than to soften their moral feeling. They soon broke out. Officers commenced their work, bringing many of them to trial for various offences. The 'triangle' was erected; the horrid 'cat' I saw with grief and pain, flourished about the station by a fellow-prisoner, appointed *flagellator*. It was soon laid upon the backs of the unhappy convicts. Then my sorrows began; I was disappointed that a milder system was not in operation. From what I conceived *probation* to be, I expected men would have been *instructed* and *drawn*, not *driven;* *encouraged*, not at once *coerced*.

"I should have told you, that for three or four months we were tolerably comfortable, owing to the influence of a pious visiting magistrate, who was over us during that brief period, and paid great attention to our spiritual interests, and instructed us, and led our worship on most sabbaths; but his stay was short. There was no flogging during his time; but he would come and talk with us, as a tender father to his children, and encourage us in every possible way, in the pursuit of useful knowledge. After he left us the scene changed! Thirty boys, incorrigible, as their conduct afterwards proved, were sent to us; and instead of being kept separate from the men, and put to suitable work, they, to my great surprise, were allowed to mix with the men, many of whom were depraved in the extreme. . . . .

"Oh, let me call forth your pity and your prayers for your fellow-creatures, destined like ourselves to exist for ever, either in heaven or in hell! They are daily passing out of time into eternity, in most cases, I fear, unprepared! . . . . Never did I feel myself so degraded, never were my feelings so hurt as now. What my mind has suffered through the wickedness of my fellow-men, I will not attempt to tell you, for I cannot: nevertheless, these things humbled me, and brought me low in the dust of self-abasement. Thank God, I believe they have induced a tender feeling for the souls of these poor creatures; and though it would be worse than useless in *me* to reason with them, or to speak to them on their danger, yet I have prayed for them, and still pray for them. With few exceptions, no man careth for their souls; our illegal conduct made us convicts, and our rulers have placed us in such circumstances as render the commission of crime easy; they put forth no counteracting influence, to bear against the evil spirit that is in man; little instruction is afforded to the mind, and that not, in my opinion, in the proper mode. I should rejoice to see Dr. Browning's plan adopted. It would be an invaluable boon to us men and women in bonds, and an extensive blessing in this community. . . . Thanks be to God, there are some pious men amongst the thousands of 'England's Exiles;' but we are all lumped together, and held to be a set of rascals and vagabonds, and are sometimes called so, by those who ought to instruct and encourage us when any good signs appear. . . . All this does us no good. I never saw a man or a boy softened and improved by flogging, or other harsh measures. A very wise man once said, you know, (and he spoke by the Spirit,) 'Though thou shouldst bray a fool in a mortar amongst wheat with a pestle, yet will not his foolishness depart from him:' and so it is with *flogging;* it only renders the feelings more callous, and the effects on the minds of others are any thing but salutary. I hope something will be done speedily for the bondmen and women in this part of the world. I am sure the present system is most ruinous both to soul and body. Habits of idleness are contracted, they assemble in groups, telling each other of the robberies and murders they have committed; and at night in the tents, the scene is truly awful. Let me ask you to pray for us, that God would, by suitable means, send out His light and His truth amongst convicts; that they may be saved in the Lord, with a present and an everlasting salvation!

"You see what I have gone through *mentally;* for what are outward inconveniences, when compared with the *distress of mind* endured in such a state of things? Transportation is *a terrible evil*, to be dreaded above all temporal evil. Under such circumstances the strongest mind becomes dejected, and the spirit broken. Oh, that men and women would take warning, and shun the commission of crime, which entails upon the offender such indescribable misery!

"Thank God, I am now in more favourable circumstances. I feel a new man in a new world, though I feel the effects of a two years' confinement in the Bush, under probation, hanging about me; but,

> The gospel bears my spirits up,
> A faithful and unchanging God
> Lays a foundation for my hope,
> In oaths, and promises, and blood!

I have now many privileges, for it is with Christian masters that I am placed, and I sit under a gospel ministry; and although I have but a prisoner's wages, I meet with kindness and encouragement. . . . ."

TESTIMONIES CONCERNING CONVICTS BROUGHT OUT BY THE "ARAB," 1834.

No. 1.—*Extract from His Excellency the Governor's Certificate.*

"It is a most gratifying duty to record the expression of the very high approbation I entertain of Dr. Browning's efforts in the discipline and reformation of the convicts during the voyage, the success of which has surpassed any thing I could have anticipated to have been accomplished in so short a period. His mode of classifying the convicts, and the plain and simple manner in which he has imparted religious instruction to them, has given an *appearance* and a *mind* to these prisoners which I have never observed on any former occasion; and I strongly recommend that the approbation of His Majesty's Government may be evinced by his being, at the earliest period, sent out in charge of another transport.

(Signed) "GEO. ARTHUR."

No. 2.—*Extract from a Report, by a Board appointed by His Excellency the Lieutenant-Governor of Van Diemen's Land, to inquire into the conduct of the Convicts by the "Arab," after they had resided five months in the Colony.*

* * * "In obedience to your letter of the 7th inst., requesting us to report upon the conduct of the convicts who arrived per *Arab*, compared with that of other prisoners, together with our opinion as to the effect produced by the discipline and system of instruction persevered in by the surgeon-superintendent during the voyage, we beg leave to state, for His Excellency's information, that, having attended the public examination of those men the day after their arrival, we were much pleased by the manner in which the convicts exhibited the instruction which they had received under Dr. Browning's tuition during the voyage; and it is really astonishing that so much could be imparted in so short a time,—particularly to a great many of them, who could neither read nor write previously to their being sent on board the vessel.

"It appeared to us that Dr. Browning had been very successful in his classification of the men, by which means a number who possessed some rudiments of learning were enabled greatly to assist the surgeon, by communicating to the more ignorant the knowledge which they themselves possessed; and the whole of the method pursued by Dr. Browning has led us to entertain the most favourable opinion of his assiduity and attention in every respect, but particularly to the religious and moral instruction of the prisoners. And we cannot avoid remarking upon the very judicious impressions made upon the minds of these prisoners by the surgeon-superintendent; and that these have not been thrown away, is best shown by the exemplary conduct of the convicts who came by the *Arab*, since their arrival.

"The superintendent of the barracks reports, that they have been invariably clean, sober, and regular, whilst at the same time none of them have yet been brought before magistrates, for punishment,—a fact which has never before occurred within the knowledge of the chief police-magistrate or principal superintendent, it usually happening that convicts, after their first landing and assignment, meet old comrades on the road to their several masters, and fall into the crime of drunkenness and other irregularities.

(Signed) "M. FORSTER, Chief Police-Magistrate.
"JOSIAH SPODE, Principal Superintendent of Convicts.
"P. PALMER, Rural Dean."

TESTIMONIES CONCERNING CONVICTS BROUGHT OUT BY THE SHIP "ELPHINSTONE," 1836.

No. 4.—*Extract from His Excellency's Certificate.*

* * * "It is truly pleasing to contemplate the gratifying results of his exertions for the reformation of the convicts placed under his charge; the peculiar excellency of the system of moral and religious education adopted on board, as set forth in his Journal, having been strongly evidenced in the general demeanour of the prisoners on landing.

* * * * * * *

(Signed) "GEO. ARTHUR."

No. 5.—*Extract referring also to the men by the "Elphinstone."*

* * * "I cannot avoid availing myself of this opportunity to draw the attention of His Majesty's Government to the very able system of education pursued by Dr. Browning during the voyage. His firm but conciliatory manner has ensured for him the respect of the convicts; and his unwearied exertions for their moral and religious improvement have called forth such evidence in their conduct, of their gratitude and esteem, as is almost incredible.

"Whilst on the voyage, men and boys were taught to read, and were so far instructed in the Scriptures as to be able to answer satisfactorily on any essential doctrine of the Christian religion. * * *

"CAPTAIN ADAMS,* of His Majesty's 28th regiment, who

---

* Nothing could be more gratifying than the *spirit* and *bearing* of this officer during the whole of the voyage. Not only did Captain Adams scrupulously guard against all interference with me, as the naval-officer in charge of the convicts, but he ever gave his most cordial co-operation. The *discipline* of the soldiers under his command, and their *general conduct* during the passage, were admirable.

commanded the guard on board the *Elphinstone*, has assured me, that such was Dr. Browning's influence over the convicts, that during the whole voyage there was not a dispute amongst them; and they appeared to dread nothing so much as giving offence to their surgeon-superintendent.

* * * * * * *

(Signed) "Geo. Arthur."

It may here be added, that when the Lieutenant Governor, Sir John Franklin, addressed the prisoners debarked from the *Earl Grey*, in the presence of a number of the colonial officers, His Excellency made frequent allusions to the superior conduct of the men who had been transported in the *Elphinstone* in 1836.

LESSONS AND SERMONS READ ON BOARD THE EARL GREY.

Lord's Day.	Lessons.	Sermons.*
Sept. 25	Ez. xxxiii. Matt. i. 18—25, ii.	Serm. i. vol. i. Text. Ps. li. 5.
Oct. 2	Gen. i. Luke i.	Serm. ii. vol. i. John iii. 16.
Oct. 9	Gen. ii. Luke ii.	Serm. iii. vol. i. Hebr. ii. 3.
Oct. 16	Gen. iii. Luke iii.	Serm. iv. vol. i. Acts xvi. 30.
Oct. 23	Gen. iv. Luke iv.	Serm. v. vol. i. 1 Tim. i. 15.
Oct. 30	Gen. vi. Luke v.	Serm. vi. vol. i. Hebr. vii. 25.
Nov. 6	Gen. vii. Luke vi.	Serm. i. vol. ii. Is. lxiv. 6.
Nov. 13	Gen. vii. Mat. xxv.	Serm. ix. vol. i. Isa. lxiv. 6.
Nov. 20	Gen. ix. 2 Peter iii.	Serm. xii. vol. i. 2 Cor. v. 10.
Nov. 27	Isa. i. John xix.	Serm. ii. vol. ii. Ephes. v. 14.
Dec. 4	Exodus xii. Acts ii.	Serm. iii. vol. ii. Matt. xxii. 5.
Dec. 11	Exodus xiv. Acts iii.	Serm. iii. vol. iv. Zech. ix. 12.
Dec. 18	Deut. iv. Acts iv.	Serm. vii. vol. i. Gal. v. 24.
Christmas day	Proper Lessons.	Serm. ii. vol. i. John iii. 16.
Jan. 1	Isa. liii. Luke xxiv.	An Address.
Jan. 8	Deut. iii. Acts ix.	Serm. x. vol. i. Phil. iv. 5.
Jan. 15	Isa. li. Matt. xiii.	Serm. viii. vol. i. Titus ii. 11, 12.

* From "Cottage Sermons," by the Rev. C. Davy, 4 vols.

Printed in Dunstable, United Kingdom